THE TWELVE METER CHALLENGES
FOR THE AMERICA'S CUP

THE TWELVE METER CHALLENGES
FOR THE AMERICA'S CUP

TEXT BY NORRIS D. HOYT

PAINTINGS AND DRAWINGS BY
ADMIRAL JOSEPH W. GOLINKIN

A *Brandywine Press* Book

E. P. DUTTON   NEW YORK

This book was edited and produced by
The Brandywine Press, Inc.
Clarkson N. Potter, President

Design by Ellen Seham
Typography by David Seham Associates, Inc.
Printed and bound in Great Britain by Cox & Wyman Ltd.

Published, 1977, in the United States by E. P. Dutton, a Division of Sequoia-Elsevier Publishing Company, Inc., New York, and simultaneously in Canada by Clarke, Irwin & Co., Ltd., Toronto and Vancouver.

Library of Congress Catalog Card Number: 77–75394
ISBN: 0-525-22450-5

10 9 8 7 6 5 4 3 2 1
First Edition

ACKNOWLEDGEMENTS

This volume really has a third creator in Ruth Fowler Golinkin, whose unfailing admiration, optimism, hospitality, and patient support activity accompanied us from the first concept to the final proofreading. The text owes much of what literary virtue it has to the rigorous analysis and tactful carping of my wife, Katherine Hoyt, my daughter, Katy Hoyt, and the publisher's editorial assistant, Anne Mooney. For the rest, I'm indebted to Jeff Spranger, Hugh Somerville, Lou d'Alpuget, Red Marston, John Aherne, Dave Phillips, Olin Stephens, Tom Clagett, Jerry Driscoll, Ted Hood, Fred Lawton, Bill Cox, Dave Pedrick, Guy Goodbody, John Rousmaniere of Yachting Magazine, Ms. Vera Robson at the NYYC, both for patience, assistance and the use of their libraries, and John Hopf for constant educational insights into the nature of the Twelve Meter contagion, its care and treatment. Finally, I doff my yachting cap to Jerry Nevins, who got me into Twelve Meter reporting in the first place.

Norris D. Hoyt

The paintings and drawings in this collaboration represent a period of fifteen years of close observation and experience through five America's Cup challenges. I am indebted to the United States Navy for granting my presence on board a destroyer in the earlier challenge, and thereafter to the United States Coast Guard for acceptance on board the eighty-two-foot cutters based in Newport. I have felt especially close to the skipper and crew of the *Point Turner*, who were attentive to my needs to observe closely and who accepted my presence as a member of the ship's company.

I am also indebted to Harry Anderson who during the long period of production maintained special interest, and who was instrumental in arranging to exhibit many of the paintings in the New York Yacht Club during the occasions of the official Cup dinners.

And finally, I am grateful to the chairmen and members of the Race Committees for the opportunities to observe from the Committee boats and the buoy tender.

Joseph W. Golinkin

5

Dedicated to the helmsmen, crews, and syndicate members of twelve meter competitors—worldwide.

CONTENTS

FOREWORD

Jo Golinkin and I first met in the summer of 1964 aboard the Coast Guard cutter *Point Turner* in the days when reporters were still allowed on Coast Guard cutters. I was broadcasting the nineteenth defense of the America's Cup between *Constellation* and the British *Sovereign* for Radio Station WADK. *Point Turner*'s skipper, Chief Boatswains Mate Sam Harris, and his crew were tactful with me, but managed to express in polite and subtle ways their skepticism at having a reporter on board their ship. I was suspect: as an ex-ensign (USNR), a schoolteacher, and worst, a small-boat sailor—a genre inspected and found wanting because of the frequent necessity to rescue such sailors from their own folly. I managed to confirm the suspicions of the crew by talking too much and asking incessant questions.

Jo, on the other hand, was clearly a member of the fraternity and a pet as well. He stood quietly on deck, smoking his pipe, observing everything with a keen eye and an unwavering concentration. He spoke when consulted, giving brief advice or precise recommendation with the

9

economy of language characteristic of artists and seamen.

Rear Admiral (ret.) Joseph Webster Golinkin has had two fine careers. As a senior naval officer, he was deeply involved in the complex mixture of command, technology, and administration that keeps a sailor alert to the nature of the sea and creative of necessity. In addition to his career in the Navy, Jo is a well-recognized American painter and visual chronicler of American sports. In 1941, he collaborated with John Kieran on a book called *The American Sporting Scene,* which incorporated every sport from boxing to fox hunting and sailing. He has been awarded two Olympic medals for Art in Relation to Sport. Jo's singular combination of intimacy and expertise with both paintbrush and sail allows him to work freely to capture line, movement, visual impact, and mood, and his chosen subject matter lends itself splendidly to his unique style.

Jo and I soon found we were bound by a common passion for twelve meters, the most beautiful of all yachts. Like women, all boats have their particular beauty, whether they are compact or leggy, lean or generous, serene or feisty. But there is an occasional feminine creation whose appeal transcends brains, beauty, or charm—a woman who symbolizes some divine elegance beyond herself—a goddess. A twelve meter, like this sort of woman, has beauty beyond ownership.

A Twelve is a very private sort of yacht. Within a stringent set of class rules, the Twelves have evolved into superperformers whose minor differences symbolize variety of function. As with great beauties, unique equipment and loving care are lavished upon them. At night their skins are polished yet again to flawless smoothness, and their trappings lovingly folded and stored against future use or meticulously recut, respliced, and restitched to new perfection. Elegantly kept, with an occasional face-lift by designer and builder, the line of their sheer and the grace of their movement is notable for years after they are introduced to society. In their season, their crews—priests and acolytes—strive together toward the perfection of ritual.

The more often we joined the Newport summers of the Twelves and the more we watched the process mature and develop, the more we realized what the New York Yacht Club (NYYC) and the contestants had managed to do—provide a suitable medium and an important ritual in our lives, a dedication to the pursuit of perfection at an elitist pinnacle of competition. The NYYC's gradual tightening of the rules, until the challenger had to represent "the technology of the country of origin," seemed to us less chauvinist protectionism than a purification of the ritual. For the America's Cup contests are just that—a ritual representation not only of complex technology, not just of numbers and materials and instruments of "the country of origin," but of a culture.

Yacht racing has always had an aura of conspicuous consumption, and certainly the days of Lord Dunraven and of J. P. Morgan were exemplary of "the richer the boy, the bigger the toy" philosophy. But "conspicuous consumption" is a sneer from sourgrapesville, and even madly spent money benefits a long chain of receivers.

Better, one might say, than squirreling it away in a swansdown mattress.

The growth to significance of the America's Cup began with Sir Thomas Lipton, the poor boy who made good. His many *Shamrocks,* supervised from the deck of his *Erin,* brought him worldwide fame and made thousands of people feel that the world did reward the busy and the lucky, and that life had grandeur. What good are the sweepstakes if there are no winners, only a miserable welfare clerk issuing you minimum sustenance? Moreover, here was a man who "had everything" who still used his organizing ability, his questing mind, and his available resources to challenge, create, and direct. Pity the poor rich! Descended from sharp minds and restless bodies that made all that money, educated subtly and well at heavily endowed schools and colleges by the brightest minds of the time, then set down in the world to spend? Or buy? Or invest? Pity the chairman of the board, risen from toolroom to office, from office to suite, and from suite into retirement—and the bright busy fire banked in him.

America's Cup contenders are the educated, the able, the powerful, seeking an arena in which to employ all their knowledge and ability—something small enough to get close to, something as real as profit and loss, something physical enough to touch. Those infected by their professors may go into politics, but those truly blessed get involved—whether in a syndicate or as sole challengers—in the America's Cup.

The Challenge and The Defense are an ultimate expression of the physical, just as poetry is the highest verbal expression of the fullness of man's experience. Trying for the Cup that no challenger has ever won, and no defender ever lost, is a kingly experience; skippering the challenger or defender is a spiritual one.

Sailing a Twelve on the first amniotic fluid, a band of brothers exists and labors within the most subtle of surfaces and the most delicate of curves. They labor in the winds and the tensions of competition in an ultimate coordination of sensitivity, rhythm, and effort. The objective is absurd—but what objective isn't? Define the ultimate and build a shrine to it. Perhaps the shrine defines more precisely than the screed. Cathedrals are more spiritual than saints or sermons; governments are more elegant than the declarations of their ministers; corporations are more lovingly structured and operated than their products or their advertising; love is lovelier than love songs.

Twelves consume much labor and few materials. They are an elegant, beautiful way to redistribute wealth to sanders, polishers, painters, mechanics, welders, yard-owners, sailmakers, chemists, mathematicians, electricians, electroniconomists, reporters, taxi drivers, airline personnel, shipowners, tax collectors, busboys, waiters, bartenders, shop owners, rental agents, chambermaids, and, on the mornings after great victories, magistrates, lawyers, and auto-body shops. Not one of these people is underprivileged or undeserving—they all work.

Twelves bring joy to viewer and doer. They make secular saints and miracle workers of those who, infected in their adolescence with the myths and legends of the class, successfully focus their lives with steady purpose and overall casualness on winning the America's Cup.

No man will win it who has not been clear in his vision, steady of purpose, and dedicated to the ultimate humility of making himself less important than his goal.

Jo and I wanted to capture the growth of this phenomenon, this gentle dedication, and to record our sense of this luring of pilgrims to Newport in quest of perfection. Jo has sought to register the flavors of the different Cup seasons—the golden drifting days of *Intrepid–Courageous*, the bitter gray afternoon of *Sovereign*'s first defeat, the beautiful symmetry of five Twelves in a consolation race, the dance of wind on water and the lean of power in hull and sail, the isolated tension of two competitors against sea and sky, the color and vision of it. I hoped to capture the sense of how the Cup grows on its communicants, from their confirmation as syndicate, crew, or helmsman; as designer, sailmaker, or project supervisor; the growth, year after year, of complex systems feeding into the total effort—new metals, new finishes, new fibers, new instruments, new tools; the slow development of that complex mix of crew—artists, technicians, analysts, walking winches—all together in a long summer season.

Perhaps the refinement of the Twelve experience shows in this factual account. The latest Twelve gimmick is a computer with twenty-nine inputs and ample readouts. Into it go the wind speed and direction, apparent wind speed and direction, boat speed, the compass course, sails used, angle of heel, air temperature, and the like. It stores memories of previous performances under similar conditions, windshift patterns, and, not surprisingly, the optimum performance of the boat as predicted by the designer's calculations and tank tests. *Courageous* alone had this computer. In a whole summer of meticulous practice and tuning, the boat achieved maximum predicted performance only in actual, very close competition.

In the Twelves, when the going is closest and the best boat and the best crew are at their peak, something happens which is projected to spectators, reporters, and painters. When *Gretel II* beat *Intrepid* by half a boatlength, the elation of the spectator fleet did not come because *Intrepid* lost or because *Gretel II* won, but because the Aussies had put it together.

Jo and I wish to share with you this unique and infinitely complex experience.

Norris D. Hoyt

Chapter One
THE NAME OF THE GAME

It is a matter for some wonder, even cynicism, that more than 125 years of challenge and some 22 matches have failed to unseat the America's Cup from its own bolt in its own room in the New York Yacht Club. It is perhaps more wonderful that, over the decades, the Club has slowly altered the rules under which the contests are held in the direction of abandoning the home team's advantages one by one. Until the Twelves, the challenger was required to sail across the ocean on her own bottom. Early challengers had to race against a whole fleet rather than a single defender.

The prospective challengers for the 1977 America's Cup will compete for an entire season against each other in the same waters sailed by the defenders. They will race in boats built to a rule which has been refined and interpreted so that the only advantage one boat can have over the other is in concept and crewing. They will be built equally, as the defender is denied the advantage of "exotic materials"—materials available only from the more complex technology of the United States.

The New York Yacht Club's early concessions toward "class" boats almost cost them the Cup. In 1934, Thomas O. M. Sopwith came across the Atlantic with *Endeavour*, the fastest "J" class boat built to date, and lost to the defending "J" boat *Rainbow*, four races to two. Had Sopwith sailed more wisely, he might actually have won four races and even a fifth. His performance, however, was consistent with a pattern of inexpertise that has plagued challengers up to the present day. He was beaten in two races, for example, by the same tactical device.

Although some challengers have outspent, outorganized, and outpublicized the winning American syndicates, they have signally failed to duplicate American techniques for developing and selecting a defender, or to equal American tactics for sailing the actual races. They have come without depth of expertise or philosophy—neophytes to a complex experience.

In 1977, for the first time, the effort of a consortium of three countries that will be challenging may, through a summer-long competitive selection process, develop skills and attitudes in an already equal challenger that will threaten American dominance of twelve meter match racing. To understand what those skills and attitudes must be and to understand why the Cup is threatened as never before, one must know the particular conditions of match racing as opposed to fleet racing, and their relationship to the general techniques of yacht racing over closed courses.

The present course for the America's Cup has evolved through successive changes by the New York Yacht Club into the "Olympic" course specified for the America's Cup by "Sailing Instructions for U.S. Trials and for Match Races," as follows:

Races shall consist of six legs. The first leg, to be approximately four and one-half nautical miles in length, shall be from the starting mark to a buoy to windward; the second leg shall be from the first mark to a mark equidistant from the starting buoy and the first mark at a point on the circumference of a circle the diameter of which is the first leg; the third leg shall be from the second mark back to the starting buoy; the fourth leg shall be from the starting buoy to the first mark; the fifth leg shall be from the first mark to the starting buoy; and the sixth leg shall be from the starting buoy to the first mark, at which the finish line shall be established.

Marks are to be left on the same hand as the starting mark.

Drawn, this course is a leg to windward, a reaching leg with the wind at forty-five degrees over the starboard quarter, a reaching leg with the wind at forty-five degrees over the port quarter, and then three legs to windward, to leeward, and to windward and the finish. Sailed, it is a minimum of 24.3 nautical miles.

If the two boats are closely matched, a race on such a course is substantially a matter of techniques and tactics, and is usually won or lost by less than a minute in a contest of more than three hours. In effect, then, design, sails, trim, and tactics must be within 1 percent of perfect to ensure competition.

The primary weapon in this war, apart from a faster boat, more experience, a better crew, and a more devious mind than your opponent, is "dirty air," or wind shadow. Wind shadow

reaches downwind from a sailboat in a long triangle, base at the boat and apex about seven times mast height directly downwind. This "dirty air" disturbs the free flow of the wind on an opponent's sails and slows him down relative to a boat with "free air." Thus a boat that starts slightly ahead and to windward of an opponent has an immediate tactical advantage—he is already laying a little wind shadow on his opponent. He can fall off, accelerate and "blanket" his opponent, forcing him to tack away. When the opponent tacks, the leader tacks on top of him, to "cover" him. In a fleet race, the leader cannot always afford to sacrifice the boatlength necessary to tack and retain a "cover" on the nearest boat, but in a match race there is only one boat to beat, so "cover" is important.

To achieve this initial control, a good start is supremely important. The windward boat has a further tactical advantage, for the rules say that the leeward boat cannot tack and force the windward boat about until it can either tack clear ahead, or tack and be fully underway before impinging upon a windward boat's course, being at the same time "able to hit the windward boat forward of the mast." A leading boat at the start thus controls the tactics on the first leg.

The rounding of the weather mark reverses the tactical control, for the trailing boat is now to windward. His downwind shadow can reach as much as ten boatlengths ahead to slow the leader, who is thus forced to maneuver to clear his air. The initiator of tactics is, of course, better prepared than the interpreter of them, and the aggressor astern may be able to force errors or hangups on the evader ahead. The following boat has the further advantage of seeing how well the leader's sail choice suits the new situation, and of anticipating a change to a slightly bolder sail. He may choose to sail a course quite wide of the next mark, and thus suck a defending leader into water and wind patterns unfavorable to him. But these tactical opportunities accrue only to a follower who is within tactical reach of a leader. In a match race between two Twelves, about thirty seconds in a fifteen-knot breeze is the outer limit of tactical reach.

Thus the tactical initiative in a match race

shifts from leg to leg, from leader to follower. Since there are only two boats, their crews will try to outmaneuver one another by luffing a windward boat head to wind, carrying an opponent over, above, or inside a mark, initiating tacking or jibeing duels, or even sailing an opponent well off the course. Anyone who used these tactics in a fleet race would lose many places to other yachts sailing the minimum distance at maximum speed.

Further tactical weapons depend on the complex rules of the International Yacht Racing Union (IYRU), and are much better understood in example than in explanation. Of course any skipper who makes the actual competition for the America's Cup will not only know the rules better than the average race committee, but will probably also have a "caller," a tactician at his ear, whose international reputation has already been honed to a fine edge in national, world, and Olympic competition.

Tactics depend upon very close quarters. There is no substitute for boat speed. Competitors for the defense or for the challenge come face to face with a cold statistic quite early: the average winner of the Cup is about a tenth of a knot faster than the previous winner. A boat built for the next race must find that elusive tenth with sails that require two months to develop proper shape and flexibility. The skipper starts with a hull whose characteristics may be quite different from any Twelve he has sailed previously, and with a crew whose already great individual skills will not be fully coordinated until extensive alterations are made in the positions of winches, cleats, platforms, and instruments. In the course of six challenges in twelve meters, it has become apparent that one summer is not enough time to achieve a boat's full potential. To achieve tactical range, the crew of a Twelve must develop her handling and equipment flawlessly. In clutch situations, it is true, both the United States and Australia have achieved unexpected tactical victories, but the series and the Cup itself are won by persistent perfectionism.

In a four-hour race, a thirty-five second superiority at any stage is an almost assured victory, yet it represents only two-tenths of 1 percent of the elapsed time. Any sail trim, steering, anticipation of wind shifts, sail handling, sail choice, mast or boom bending, or sheeting angle that is not initially more than 99 44/100 percent right can lose the race. Every new boat arriving for the trials at Newport faces the local conditions, the technology of the new challenge, and the training of a different crew. The skipper and his syndicate face a long process. They must practice, tune, recut, alter, and adapt until they bring their boat within tactical range of old boats with several years of experience.

Much of the fascination that continues to bring challenger and defender to the America's Cup is the challenge of developing, of getting it all together. Losing one round is not the end, as *Weatherly*, eliminated in her first try, found out when she won the Cup on her second. The newest ideas are not always the best—*Intrepid* demonstrated this when she beat the newest and latest S & S *Valiant* and eked out a close series against *Gretel II.*

In the summer of 1974 both sides had sail lofts and resident sailmakers; both sides had computer experts, project managers with professional accreditation in hull, rig, and aerodynamic design, and a solid herd of world-class sailors to handle lines, winches, and sails. Three designers followed Twelves that were practicing, day after day, in "chase boat" motor cruisers, noting angle of heel, set of sail, turbulence of wake, cross flow under the transom, and waterline trim. They conveyed their suggestions to the practicing crews by CB radio on private crystals. Ballast was shifted, decks were pierced for new equipment and old holes plugged; welders, painters, sanders, and sailmakers worked through the dark hours. Chefs and den mothers managed menus and social obligations. Every Twelve was hauled and hand-polished at least once a week. *Intrepid,* the wooden semifinalist, was hauled every day to keep her light and dry. She was hand-polished daily by her crew, her skipper, and even her designer and syndicate managers. When *Mariner* was away being rebuilt, her full crew spent two days polishing her two masts. While *Mariner's* crew polished aluminum, *Intrepid* and *Courageous* were polishing techniques in a race, won by six seconds, in which the lead was exchanged six times.

In the development process, close competition is in no way guaranteed, nor is early failure any indication of future performance. A Twelve, unlike a toothbrush, does not arrive in a sanitary package ready for instant use. Like a child, she must be taught everything, her clothes must be fitted, and she must be understood in great depth before she can be wisely guided through a difficult adolescence.

Sails, for example, are exceedingly subtle items on a Twelve's agenda. This is an area in which major development is still to come. It may take an entire summer to develop one perfect twelve meter mainsail. Modern synthetics introduce a vast array of variables. DuPont, for example, makes several hundred kinds of Dacron filaments, and sailcloth makers use different mixes of these for different weights of cloth. On the usual twelve meter mainsail, about a ten-ounce cloth is used. The threads running parallel with the seams are mixed for more elasticity than the threads running vertical to the seams. Since there is some residual stretch in all fibers, a new sail will need to complete its stretch before it finds its true shape.

The nature of Cup racing makes it mandatory to have maximum area in the mainsail, as the mainsail on a Twelve is really main, and not the scrimy slice of pie it is on an ocean racer. The Twelve has only a three-quarter foretriangle, and her main, unlike her genoas, cannot be replaced during a race to suit changing conditions. It must be full for reaching and running, and flat for working to windward. The location of its maximum fullness (draft) must vary for varying conditions. Since the mast can be only eighty-two feet high, and the boom, fixed solidly at the tack for maximum area at all times, must clear the helmsman's hands on the wheel, the mainsail area is limited to a triangle between the tack at the front of the boom, the outhaul at the after-end of the boom, and the band at the top of the mast. These three fixed points take almost the entire strain of the mainsail. The luff of a twelve meter main goes up in a slot which

supports it against fore-and-aft strain, but tension in the luff is increased or decreased by the "Cunningham Hole," a stainless-steel grommet in the luff-tabling about three feet above the boom. Through this grommet a line pulls down from a dead end on one side of the mast to a winch on the other. Once maximum tension is taken on the Cunningham, the sail is loose along the boom and maximum stretch and distortion occurs at the Cunningham, the masthead, and the clew.

A twelve meter mainsail is some nine hundred square feet and, going to weather, supports a strain of three to five pounds per square foot. The mainsheet, powerfully winched down, puts a great deal of the strain on the boom end and the reinforced cloth of the clew and the unreinforced cloth along the leach. This two-ton load stretches the cloth panels more than the leach-tabling (which is three times as strong as a single thickness of cloth), and thus stretches the leach end of the panels more than the middle or the luff. So, by the time the sailmaker has recut to compensate for residual stretch and worked the sail through two months of patient development, the seams at the leach have a gentle "S" curve, and a subtle downward frown near the Cunningham. A mainsail which looked as casual as a lunchbag at the end of the first week of sailing now looks almost as elegant to the crew as their competitor's virtually perfect sail.

Once the main is satisfactory, the sailmakers and sailtrimmers must develop four or five spinnakers, a few reachers, seven or eight genoas and random tallboys, spinnaker staysails, bloopers, and perhaps a heavy and a light-weather main.

Once these sails please the professional eye, their relationship to one another must be determined, and this relationship can be subtle indeed. For example, *Bolero*, a seventy-two-foot ocean racer about the size of a Twelve, had a No. 1 genoa that would take her higher and faster to weather than any other sail. It reached its perfect trim when it was between three and four inches off the lower spreader. When she raced, she had one man calling the trim and men on the coffee-grinder constantly taking it in and letting it out to that trim, even on a four-day

race to Bermuda. As the sail grew older and weaker it was sent to its original sailmaker to be duplicated, and in two attempts, he failed to equal it. But then she got a new mainsail, and the old No. 1 had no magic with the new main—one of the newer ones outperformed it.

The relationships between sails depend on a multitude of factors: the strength of the wind, the angle of heel, the temperature, the sea condition, the angle of the apparent wind, and the lead-drag angle* of the boat. It takes literally hundreds of hours of sailing to get the precise trim for every condition. No science can exist as long as the record is merely descriptive. The sail trimmers must start from precise numbers and number-relationships, and translate these abstract concepts gradually into tangible, practical actions. The crew glues numbered measuring strips on the deck along sheet leads, colored

---

*The angle between the course made good and the compass course, normally two to three degrees. A boat must have its bow to windward of its rudder-skeg to get a lift from bow and keel conformation.

bands appear on sheets, compass roses are painted forward and aft beside the cockpit, and halyards are benchmarked with tapes. The navigator makes endless notes which he collates nightly. As definite conclusions emerge they are fed into a computer and the skipper's mind to generate answers regarding trim, relationships, and what sails to discard.

Before a Twelve is built, her naval architect runs thousands of dollars worth of tank tests with models, comparing predicted (estimated?) performances with the performances of other Twelves built from other designs by his shop, and makes reasonably accurate predictions of optimum possible speeds for the hull with given sails and given wind velocities. Once the basic statistics are established, basic truths about hull design and sailmaking become part of the computer's memory banks, and young naval architects, working out their apprenticeships in older offices, absorb about 95 percent of established knowledge about hull and sail design. With the first 95 percent common knowledge in the trade, the last 5 percent is all-important.

The computer on board was inevitable. It began to develop during the last two challenges from the simple "black box" on *Gretel II* to its successor on *Southern Cross,* and to Dick McCurdy's more elaborate and better performing gray suitcase on *Courageous,* known as "Sidney Greybox." With inputs from anemometer, compass, wind direction, apparent wind direction, speed through water, angle of heel, and various memories of predicted performance, sail trim, specific sails, sheet positions, sheet tensions, shroud and halyard tension, and who-but-the-navigator-knows-what-else, "Sidney" compared results day by day, and changes were made accordingly.

Some of the 1977 Twelves were completed almost a year in advance of the Cup season; many of the older Twelves underwent extensive redesign and modification after their initial season. A month or a year of such preliminaries prepares a boat, her sails, her skipper and his crew for the only test that really counts—a race against another Twelve. No matter how elegant the sails or how optimistic the performances predicted, the elusive tenths of 1 percent get very big. One hull that tests as a breakthrough and sails very well under full sail comes to a virtual halt each time it goes through a tack and must be redesigned. Sails that look perfect turn out to be slower than the competition's. The mast of one contender will bend more than the mast of another, and she gains a few seconds downwind every time she cranks it three feet beyond the vertical over the bow. Another discovers that she cannot point within three degrees of her competition, but that she can walk away from them when driven off for speed.

So sails are recut, ballast is shifted, hulls are shaved a bit here and built out a bit there, rudder sizes and shapes are altered, and gamesmanship rears its ugly head. If you have a maximum genoa that will beat a fellow contender's maximum genoa, do you let him realize it and recut, or do you hastily change it for a sail you are less sure of, thus keeping a competitive edge in the bank until you need to draw upon it? Only the final selection trials, at the end of August, are decisive.

As the summer goes on, two boats emerge as prime contenders, and a few superior sailors move from the eliminated boats to those still competing, along with a few superior sails. Each competitor choreographs its own precise ballet for movement from job to job of its crew during tack, luff, or jibe. "An American in Paris" is not "Swan Lake," and, for a while, people bump into each other because Jim is three inches broader in the bottom than Fred, whom he replaced. Worse, Jim brought with him a really useful idea for a change in the deck layout. In August, syndicate members look on in horror as their million-dollar investments come back to the shipyard and the crew drill holes and move gear. But one hangup on a tack or a takedown can cost the race, and five seconds saved on a set can win it. The variables now account for less than a tenth of 1 percent.

Meanwhile, gear that has been painstakingly developed, benchmarked, and fondly maintained is wearing out. The winches are rebuilt and rotated, of course, on a regular schedule. But the sheets, backstays, vangs, guys, and downhauls, stretched to their final dimensions and suitably marked, have to be renewed. Can we afford one last race with the old ones we know?—it's an important one, and either a mistake with new stuff or a gear failure with the old stuff could blow it.

Complications do not end here. The elaborate notes that strategists and managers have been making all summer now produce results. Winds, for example, are not wholly predictable, but they have general characteristics that are. A summer sou'wester in Newport (the prevailing wind) can almost be programmed. Mornings are still and clear—jewellike and beautiful. A Twelve is towed out to the racing grounds around 1100 as the light northerly of the night is fading, and the sou'wester is starting little ruffles and catspaws on the water. By 1300, and earlier in the summer, it is blowing a pleasant eight to ten knots from something south of southwest. It will often freshen in midsummer, reaching eighteen to twenty knots by 1600, and as it freshens it moves a little west of southwest. Until it gets past southwest, it will phase south—swing four or five

degrees back to the south for a few minutes, and then return to where it was. The intervals are reasonably regular. In late afternoon, it phases westward, and the periods are more sustained. A Twelve that correctly anticipates this phasing can tack into an advantage and tack back to an advantage. A boat for whom a phase is a knock, even if it is of only two minutes' duration, will lose a boatlength or more per miscalculation. So there's another one for the magic box or the navigator. What recorded observations will allow one to predict New England's more subtle variations of wind? Given temperature, wind velocity, time of day, bearing and distance from Point Judith, can an electronic computer be programmed to give a prediction? I don't know that this happens, because winners seldom show more than openers, but it's the type of question that has to be asked.

The point then, of this long preamble to the tale of the Twelves: The America's Cup Race in the present vehicle is a marvelously complex experience, and cannot possibly be approached in any other kind of boat. "J" boats were too large and too expensive, and the state of the art was not far enough advanced for them to offer the possibilities of intricate development which make the closed-course match race such a challenge to designer, sailor, athlete, and planner. Previous America's Cup racing in mastodons under acres of canvas was spectacular and arrogantly expensive, but it was bought and paid for, and had as little meaning to the nabobs or syndicates supporting it as the diamonds in the Queen's crown have to her own productive labor.

Since the Twelves became America's Cup yachts, the lure of the contest has grown; people who have participated as crew or as syndicate members have gotten into the planning, the exploration of new alleys of attack, the selection and training of personnel, and the tactics of every race as deeply as spectators, coach, and team are involved with the Boston Celtics or the Miami Dolphins. To have sailed on a Cup defender is a profound and patriotic experience, encapsulating at a peak of intensity the characteristics of the American nation: the fascination

with a constantly developing technology; the work ethic (if you work harder than the other fellow—bust your butt trying—you can't miss the top); the shared experience of frontier, war, and college rolled into "one crowded hour of glorious life"; and, beat the drum slowly, the sad, sweet awareness (*haec olim memenisse . . .*) that obsolescence, crouched in grim repose, awaits even this triumph, this matchless band of brothers!

The Twelves improve slightly between each defense and the next. Roughly, for each million spent by American syndicates on twelve meter development, the speed of a current Twelve is improved by about five-hundredths of a knot. Significantly, the cockpit instruments, which used to register speed in tenths, now register in hundredths of a knot. The average speed for winners has increased almost three-quarters of a knot since *Columbia,* nineteen years younger than the refurbished *Vim,* battled for the defender's slot in 1958 and won by seconds in the closest series until *Intrepid–Courageous* 1974. Every five-hundredths of a knot is worth two minutes a race, and two minutes exceed the margin of the closest selection races. The improvement is not in hull design alone. Rather it is a long string of minor technical advances which combine to produce better handling, better sail-carrying ability, streamlining, better sails and sailcloth, and improved sailing techniques.

As the Twelves get faster, they get more subtle, and depend for their competitive edge more and more on the most sophisticated computer of all, the human brain. However fast your boat, and however well-trained and practiced your crew, in the last analysis close competition depends on exact decisions and a seat-of-the-pants instinct that tells the helmsman, as he fine-tunes to the wind after each tack, each jibe, and each rounding, whether his boat is making 99.5 percent of her potential. If he must experiment with his complex array of cockpit instruments and computer readouts, he's losing against a competitor who does not.

This hard fact brings up a final consideration: the helm of a winning boat must be in the hands of a man who has made sailing his whole life. Sailors and sailboats abound in America. Children who win consistently at their yacht club or public classes go on to sail for their school teams, for their colleges, and for the sailmaker or boatbuilder with whom they take jobs. One of America's great sailmakers turned down a Rhodes Scholarship for an apprenticeship; *Courageous'* two helmsmen were, respectively, the editor of *Yachting,* and the worlds's most famous sailmaker, designer, and winning skipper. These are people whose whole lives have been informed by the endless fascination of sailing.

And so the question with which we open our examination of the Era of the Twelves is this: can any other country field the technology, the attitudes, and the number of helmsmen for whom sailing is, and has been—since their age came in single digits—a string of triumphs? Can it get them to compete, in Twelves, among themselves, until the man and the hour come together? Will the United States ever lose the America's Cup?

Chapter Two
NEW DIMENSIONS
Columbia vs. *Vim*

Weatherly vs. *Gretel*

Between 1937 and 1950, World War II and the postwar economy made racing for the America's Cup in the 143-foot "J" class boats less than reasonable. In the 1950s, with a few nudges from Great Britain, the present generation of the New York Yacht Club began to contemplate the dormant America's Cup. The catalyst was Olin Stephens, a singularly successful, young, yacht designer.

Stephens was the first designer to utilize the towing tank successfully. In 1931 his friend, frequent shipmate, and close collaborator, Dr. Kenneth S. M. Davidson, constructed a 131-foot-long tank at Stevens Institute and towed meticulously shaped models (0.9 inch to a foot) in it to determine relative resistance, wave-making characteristics, laminar flow and separation, and other considerations a naval architect takes into account. On a carriage equipped with the instrumentation, the models were towed at various angles of heel, pitch, and lead-drag angle. The first model was of Davidson's own boat, *Gimcrack,* and the first statistics against which other boats were tested were called "the *Gim-*

AMERICA'S CUP—1962
"Australians off Brenton Lightship"
*Gretel leads Vim in practice on a bright, southwest day. Vim was
secured by Sir Frank Packer as a "trial horse" for Alan Payne's new
design. The early Twelves had their winches on deck, halyard
winches on the mast, and a canvas collar around the mast to prevent
jib sheets from catching during tacks. Halyard tension was therefore
not frequently manipulated.*
*In this picture, as the morning breeze builds and the land clouds
march from Point Judith across Newport's approach channel, the
Brenton Reef Lightship, later replaced by Brenton Tower, appears
for the last time in America's Cup history.*

crack constants." Tank testing is relative, rather than absolute; the scatter is greater as the true size of the hull increases. Nothing is really certain about the tank's dicta, and an architect with extensive experience in all sizes of sailing craft is not likely to believe the tank with heart and soul. Its current director, Pierre DeSaix, described it as "a confused midwife rather than a faithless mistress."

Stephens's success with the tank was a product of his approach to it. While Davidson was developing tank techniques and statistics, Olin Stephens and his brother, Roderick Stephens, Jr., brought the complexities of yacht design, wide experience in sailing, and the "factory team" concept to an unprecedented dominance of class and ocean racing. Olin's "feel" for the reality of performance is rarely seduced by mere tank statistics. His brother Rod's systematic supervision of every detail of rig, equipment, and construction, and his ruthless development of crew performance and sail-handling techniques brought a new intensity to offshore and closed-course racing. The triumvirate of Rod, Olin, and

Doc Davidson burst upon the yachting world and took command.

Their early success with *Dorade, Stormy Weather,* and *Edlu* was so great that Harold S. (Mike) Vanderbilt, skipper and syndicate head of all "J" boat defenders, brought Olin and W. Starling Burgess together for collaboration on the final and ultimate "J" boat, *Ranger.* She beat all the other "J's" so decisively that she probably did as much as the postwar economy to make "J" boat racing obsolete. When the Davidson–Stephens triumvirate went into the six and twelve meter classes, *Goose* dominated the Sixes, and in England, where the Twelves were most often raced, Vanderbilt's *Vim* lost once in twenty-nine races (because she went aground).

The appeal of the Twelves to the New York Yacht Club was initially *Vim's* design superiority in 1938 and '39; the appeal of the Twelves to the first challengers under the new rules, the English, was that they had been designed and raced primarily in British waters. As far as Olin Stephens can remember, no "member of the group instrumental in changing the rule" had ever owned a Twelve, "although a number of those involved were thoroughly familiar with the boats." There were, by the way, three Stephens Twelves being raced in Long Island Sound by 1939.

A committee to consider the matter of smaller America's Cup contenders was called together by Harry Sears, Commodore of the Club, in May 1956. He suggested that the Deed of Gift be given a revised interpretation which would allow twelve meters to take part in the America's Cup. The change required the approval of the Supreme Court of the State of New York, and Luke Lockwood, Secretary of the New York Yacht Club and a senior partner of the law firm of Carter, Ledyard, and Milburn, handled the active part of the legal proceedings.

The Committee, in their combined wisdom, realized that the twelve meter rule (The International Rule) defined a yacht sufficiently useless except for class racing to preclude random development. Under any ocean-racing rule, boats spring out of the boondocks and come to the line with no rules committee ever having heard of them. They conform to the letter of the rule, but take gross advantage of it. They are too many and too frequent to block off in advance. Once a loophole is clear, the rule is changed rather than reinterpreted, and with every change in the basic mathematics, more doors open, more variants erupt from the computer, and more changes ensue. Finally, dangerously specialized and uncomfortable boats bring the current rule under disapproval, and a new rule starts the game all over again.

The tab on a current Twelve has risen from half a million in 1958 to more than a million today, and nobody, under the International Rule, wants to finance a surprise. The Cup Races are (since 1970) at least three years apart, and the challenges and defenses are two or more years in the planning. The resulting yachts are closely matched, technologically mature, remarkably equal machines. The races are a test of management, skill, and selective adaptation. The press, sociologically oriented theorists, and self-appointed critics who clamor for "a yacht that can be used for something else," or "open-

AMERICA'S CUP—1962
"Parade of Spinnakers"
Five spinnakers bloom in the NYYC Cruise races out of Padanarum
in a Buzzard's Bay chop. Gretel (far right), to weather of Nefertiti,
is getting some sense of the tactics and responses of American
skippers. Later, to defend against just such a learning exercise,
challengers would not be invited on "the Cruise." Columbia (far
left), is sharpening to keep out of the wind shadow of Weatherly and
Easterner. Her all-white spinnaker would later become a custom
rather than an exception. It keeps the opposition from instant
recognition of spinnaker weight.

36

ing the America's Cup to ocean racers or an Olympic class," are off the beam. The New York Yacht Club's choice of Twelves is a masterstroke. However mildly motivated it was by their certainty of America's current superiority, competition in Twelves contains the lure of eventual equality at an elitist pinnacle of competition.

In December 1956, Commodore Henry Sears applied to the Supreme Court of the State of New York to get the Deed of Gift of the America's Cup changed to admit Twelves to the competition. A Deed of Gift, like a will or a trust, can be altered only by proper legal procedure, and, in 1958, the deed was changed in two respects. First, the minimum waterline was set at forty-four feet, and second, the challenger did not have to sail from her native country on her own bottom. The Club had abandoned some of its advantages—more, actually, than it knew. But their design advantage was to prove initially unassailable.

The nineteen-year-old *Vim* was thoroughly refurbished in 1957 by her then current owner, Captain John Matthews, and sent to the 1958

wars with a superb crew including his two sons, "Bus" Mosbacher (who would, subsequently, win the Cup twice), Dick Bertram, Buddy Bombard (who would sail on three defenders), Ted Hood (whose sails would power all subsequent defenders, as they powered *Vim*) and Jakob Isbrandtson (whose son would crew on *Courageous* when Hood skippered her to a win in 1974). From the start of the Twelves, the America's Cup virus has caused lasting infections.

Three new contenders for the 1958 defense were built, two of whom would win the Cup: *Columbia, Weatherly,* and *Easterner.* This wealth of defenders set a pattern which, however plain to students of yachting history, was apparently beyond the comprehension of challengers before 1977. The actual Cup Races were often pointless—*Sceptre* lost four straight races to *Columbia* without ever having been competitive. Yet the first American Selection Trials established three principles for winning the Cup: first, a summer of intense competition is needed to develop a Twelve to her potential; second, ruthless weeding and change in equipment, crew, and helmsman may be necessary; and finally, Hood sails perform better on a Twelve than any other sails to date.

Let us consider the last first. Hood's father, known widely as "the Professor," made his success in the textile industry and gave Ted a set of looms in 1952 to weave his own cloth. Ted Hood resembles a vaudeville-turn-in-England Yankee. Gaunt, bulbnosed, and monosyllabic, he is almost totally uninformative in a perfectly agreeable way. He has been a successful sailor since his childhood. His absorption in the sport, together with his father's business, logically led him into sailmaking and yacht design. Today, Hood Sails is a worldwide organization, and Hood himself designed, built, and made the sails for defense contender *Nefertiti*. Boats designed by Hood have won almost every major ocean race and have their own highly individual character, which is occasionally unfathomable to anyone but Ted. Hood's lean concentration and leaner conversation convey the impression that something more subtle and private than tangible evidence talks to him. *Vim*, nineteen years younger than *Columbia* from Olin Stephens's board, was the first Twelve using Hood sails which also employed Hood as sailtrimmer. Since then every successful Twelve has had a resident sailmaker, every winner, Hood sails.

Vim came to the trials with the best crew on the course, with a boat whose total capabilities were well known to the crew, and with a skipper whose mystique closely resembled Hood's, Emil (Bus) Mosbacher. Mosbacher, Cornelius (Corny) Shields, and Arthur (Artie) Knapp were helmsmen respectively on *Vim, Columbia,* and *Weatherly*. All three were old rivals in the hottest class on Long Island Sound, International One Designs. Mosbacher and Shields had extensive experience offshore and in larger boats. Mosbacher, in particular, had a gift for "putting a boat together" and "finding the groove." Shields was systematic and sensitive—always most dangerous at the end of a series when his knowledge of local weather, local currents, and his competitors' habits had become comprehensive. Knapp's expertise was boat speed—trimming weight, tuning the rig, coordinating

AMERICA'S CUP—1962
"False Tack"
On the first leg of the first Gretel–Weatherly *race, Sturrock, below
a torpedo range buoy, luffs up toward Mosbacher in a false tack. His
crew, to give the act realism, man the coffee-grinders. Mosbacher,
unbluffed, drives through Gretel's wind under the watchful eye of
Henry Mercer's* Blue Jacket, *which leads the spectator fleet behind
the Coast Guard cutter.*

Mercer's yacht flies the syndicate flag for Weatherly. *A shipping
magnate, Merger financed Weatherly's building and first campaign,
and was joined for her successful defense by Cornelius Walsh and
Arnold Frese.*

the crew—and aggressive tactics. Briggs Cunningham, sharing *Columbia*'s helm with Shields, was a famous innovator and excellent helmsman.

The most beautiful of the three was the varnished *Easterner,* designed by Ray Hunt and from Marblehead rather than Long Island Sound. She was designed for, built by, and crewed by Chandler Hovey and his family. Like *Weatherly,* she was the first Twelve off her designer's board, and, like *Weatherly,* had been built without the close and experienced supervision of Rod Stephens. *Easterner* and *Weatherly* were characterized more by excellent craftsmanship than by the search for minimum hull weight. For example, *Weatherly*'s frames were heavier than Lloyd's minimum requirements for scantlings, and the bars for keeping sails in her sailbins were of one-inch-thick and six-inch-wide mahogany. *Columbia*'s sail bins were of aluminum tubing (and, ten years later, Dacron webbing) and her frames were minimal and laminated, as laminated wood is eight times as strong as steam-bent wood of the same dimensions.

All the hull shapes were tank-tested by Professor Davidson. As always, the results were kept secret from rivals. When the information was no longer critical, it was revealed that *Easterner* had the highest potential, followed in order by *Columbia, Weatherly,* and *Vim.* The trials did not turn out that way. Artie Knapp spent much of the summer chipping wood out of *Weatherly.* The Hoveys led, off and on, but too rarely at the finish, despite their Hood sails.

Thanks to her crew, Hood sails, and tactics, *Vim* was a consistent winner in the observation races and the preliminary trials. *Columbia,* with Cunningham and Shields alternating at the helm, gradually refined her sails, which were made and trimmed by Colin Ratsey, tuned her rig, took off her lifelines, relocated her cleats, discovered that her small spinnakers were more effective than her big ones, and eventually managed in the final five races to eke out a three-to-two margin over *Vim.* Mosbacher won the start in the penultimate race, but Cunningham, with a start he had dreamed up and saved for the key hour, won the final start and the race—even though *Vim* pulled ahead *twice.*

42

If there is truth in the tank, the *Vim–Columbia* series had its message. The second-best hull barely beat the worst hull. But the boat with the least potential had the most experienced crew, the most highly developed sails, and the best skipper. Slightly behind her, the second-best boat, inexperienced and undeveloped, had excellent minds and a large pool of talent. Tempered in the heat of intense competition, she gained a shallow margin of experience and approached her potential.

The challenger's effort was, by comparison, absurd. *Sceptre* arrived at the starting line having had no real competitive experience, steered by a good sailor with no competitive background in boats comparable in size to a Twelve. Her syndicate managers were not hardnosed members of the American yachting and financial community, but a group of kindly, elegant, elderly British gentry, whose sense of loyalty and gallantry was infinitely superior to their sense of competition and their critical understanding of boat speed.

The American effort had an advantage over the British that went beyond superior design and technical vocabulary. It was run, as one of the Hoveys was later to remark, "like IBM." To those of us who know the tireless consideration of Tom Watson and his followers, this remark had the earmarks of Bostonian parochialism. Its intent was to indicate a ruthless pragmatism that went beyond having a bash with laughing fellow-rovers—a pragmatism which maximized effectiveness in spite of loyalties and commitments. A glance at the syndicate of any America's Cup defender will show an aggressive group with management backgrounds, and, perhaps more important, a group whose members have had immediate experience at crewing, skippering, and racing their own ocean-going yachts. One thinks of Gil Verney's *Sea Lion*, Walter Gubelmann's *Windigo*, George Moffett's *Guinivere*, Pat Haggerty's *Bay Bea* and *Beyondan*; one also thinks of Haggerty's Texas Instruments, Tom Clagett's coal mines, and Jack Dorrance's Campbell's Soup.

"Like IBM," the American syndicate firmly advised the syndicate manager, and the whole preparation of *Columbia*'s effort was accompanied

AMERICA'S CUP—1962
"Spinnaker Finish"

Mosbacher's closest win over Gretel *came in the fourth race, with the count at two to one in* Weatherly's *favor. After leading* Gretel *off on a reach, Mosbacher's sharper angle for the finish line allowed him to eke out a twenty-six-second win over a rapidly gaining* Gretel. *The competitive advantage that accrues to a closely following boat in a downwind finish gave* Gretel *one win and one almost-win. It also gave the NYYC palpitations, and thenceforth the course would be the standard six-leg Olympic pattern with a finish to windward.*

44

by the compilation of statistics. When *Columbia* went to the mark for the first twelve meter defense, she knew exactly what each sail would do and exactly how to trim it. Significantly, in the first race against *Sceptre*, where the wind was two to six knots at the start and ten to twelve at the finish, *Columbia* used two genoas, *Sceptre* at least four.

Since *Vim* versus *Columbia* set the pattern for subsequent American defenses and infected at least two subsequent winning skippers with the America's Cup fever, let's look at the dimensions of the campaign for selection. *Columbia* raced 692 miles between June and September, 1958. By the end of the observation races in June and the preliminary trials in July, *Vim* had won twenty-five times and had lost ten times, *Columbia* had won twenty-one times and lost fourteen times, *Weatherly* had won thirteen times and lost twenty, and *Easterner* had won nine times and lost twenty-four. *Vim* had come up with a "bendy" boom to improve mainsail shape, and, on *Columbia*, in an attempt to get a perfect helmsman and a tactician, Olin Stephens, Palmer Sparkman, and Corny Shields were variously on and off the crew.

On the fourth of September, the selection committee narrowed the competition to *Vim* and *Columbia*. On the fifth, *Columbia* won by four minutes and twenty-one seconds, after *Vim* had a bad jib hangup on the first leg. On the sixth, in a moderate breeze, *Vim* was ahead by 1:09 at the first mark, by 0:12 at the end of the second, and fell behind until *Columbia* lost her spinnaker on the next to last leg. *Vim* won by three boatlengths—ten seconds. The eighth was windy, some twenty-two knots, and *Columbia* was at her best, winning impressively by 2:22. *Vim* doused her spinnaker in the water for at least a minute of that loss.

In commenting on their elimination, *Easterner* had been a little bitter at Ray Hunt's early departure from the crew. Hunt, a master of acidulous tact, riposted: "Time brings on an age that diminishes accurate observation and aggressive thinking. Perhaps I have reached such an age."

Meanwhile, Vic Romagna had been borrowed

for *Columbia*'s crew from the eliminated *Weatherly*, and on the ninth of September, *Vim* evened the score, winning by 1:35 from *Columbia*, who lost time with a broken winch. On the tenth, *Columbia* got a poor start, caught *Vim*, but was carried past the first mark by Mosbacher. The wind picked up from eighteen to twenty-two knots. *Columbia* split tacks from *Vim* and drove off for speed on the second windward leg. She finally passed *Vim*, and won by 2:49. Time was running out, and when the final trial race was held on the twelfth of September, Briggs Cunningham took over the helm from Corny Shields. He won the start and was ahead by a minute at the windward mark. The second leg, a leeward one, ended with *Vim* ahead by eight seconds, the third with *Columbia* ahead by eight seconds after two changes of the lead during the leg, and the final downwind leg with *Columbia* winning by twelve seconds. The Committee had seen enough. *Columbia* didn't panic when behind, had the speed and the skills to get ahead, and finally emerged triumphant over her nineteen-year-old predecessor.

On *Vim*, Bus Mosbacher and Ted Hood were incurably infected by America's Cup fever. If the virus goes only helmsman-deep, it can be cured in two or three campaigns. If it penetrates both designer *and* helmsman, it can be lasting, and even terminal. Between 1958 and 1962, Mosbacher raced extensively with *Easterner*, hoping, one suspects, that he'd be offered her as a platform for the next selections. Chandler Hovey somehow couldn't bring himself to conduct a campaign supported outside the family, or run at the intensity and expense and committee-management level of *Vim*'s effort. Mosbacher loved *Easterner* and the Hoveys, but knew the cost of winning and made his move to *Weatherly*, even though he knew *Easterner* had a greater potential in the test tank.

In everything but design *Weatherly* was the ideal boat. Shipping magnate Henry Mercer felt more new boats were needed to make the defense of the America's Cup reasonably certain. He turned the job of designing, crewing, and campaigning a Twelve over to his old friend and designer Phil Rhodes, admonishing him, "Get

AMERICA'S CUP—1964
"Consolation Race"
On the Sunday, September 13, between the trials and the America's
Cup Races, a constellation of eliminated Twelves split tacks for
Commodore Harry Morgan's "Consolation Cup." The skippers of
Nefertiti *(Aus.)*, Columbia *(U.S.)*, Easterner *(U.S.)*,
American Eagle *(U.S.) and* Norsaga *(England), represent, to*
date, nineteen years of America's Cup fever. Columbia
won this race.

48

the best builder and select the finest crew. And if we don't win, don't worry."

Rhodes had done well. *Weatherly* tested better than *Vim*, but she didn't have fully developed sails and a practiced crew, and she never caught up. In the years between races, Mercer kept improving *Weatherly*. Al Luders was called in for consultation, and he ran more tests, chopped two feet off the stern, added ballast, and improved the keel shape. In the passage of time, *Weatherly* developed a truly excellent set of sails and had more on order. Given Mercer's free hand, Mosbacher had vastly improved his chances of defending. What he could not know was that the boat he had chosen was not as fast, potentially, as the challenger, Sir Frank Packer's *Gretel*.

Columbia's defeat of *Sceptre* had been so tacticless, total, and overwhelming that it had put the New York Yacht Club's suspicions to sleep. A challenger that goes down the tube in four straight races by margins of 7:44, 11:42, 8:20, and 6:52 hardly starts the adrenalin surging. So when Sir Frank Packer, whose bluster and brass was a stalking horse for a mind as devious and sly as a barrel of snakes, asked permission to use the towing tank of Stevens Institute (there was no tank in Australia), to use American sailcloth (no Dacron was made in Australia), and to use *Vim* (purchased under someone else's name) as a trial horse (for a set of proven lines?) the Committee somnolently agreed.

Gretel was therefore designed by Alan Payne with the full assistance of Olin Stephens's *Vim* and of Pete DeSaix and the tank at Hoboken. And while the exact statistics of other tests are never revealed to competing architects, DeSaix does tell the competing architect whether or not he's "in the ball park." What this means is difficult to specify precisely, but my guess is that no hull is in the ball park that is predicted to be 1 percent slower than the top current hulls. So Payne's results were at least in the same park as Luders–Rhodes, and, as it turned out, he was actually closer to home plate.

Meanwhile, E. Ross Anderson, Commodore of the Boston Yacht Club, was tuned in to the fact that the U.S. was coming into a considerably sophisticated challenge with no new Twelves. During the cocktail hour which preceded a dinner held at the Boston Yacht Club in October 1961, Ross remarked that he saw no reason why a native effort from Marblehead couldn't get into the ring and have a shot at the Cup. At dinner that night, he announced his decision to enter the fray, and his choice of designer was Ted Hood.

In addition to being a sailmaker, Hood had been designing boats and doing very well both locally and on NYYC cruises. He had never designed a Twelve, however, and had no access to the lines of a successful one. Hood took as an assistant Britton Chance, Jr., a tremendously talented young designer with extensive experience in tank testing. Together the two worked night and day and finally, in January 1962, they got out the lines of *Nefertiti*. The new boat, obviously very fast in heavy air, had a bit too much wetted surface on the keel, and rather more beam than any ther Twelve. Her foretriangle was larger than average (indicating the direction Hood would move ocean racing in subsequent years). She was a very fast boat, and when the wind blew she won. Her success was aided by Don MacNamara, the "stormy petrel" of Boston, an aggressive, hopelessly explosive, tactless, and highly talented helmsman. His blunt animadversions on the intelligence of the NYYC's Race Committee eventually got him ruled off the course.

Nefertiti was launched in May, and at the end of July she had scored ten wins and two losses to *Weatherly*'s seven wins and four losses. But *Weatherly*'s two wins were by 5:43 and 4:24 over *Nefertiti*, in light airs, and *Nefertiti*'s two wins over *Weatherly* were by 0:43 and 0:54 in brisk winds. *Easterner* won once, over *Weatherly*, and *Columbia* only four times, three over *Easterner*.

Throughout August, the wind never got up to twelve, and in light-air day after light-air day, MacNamara's patience and *Nefertiti*'s chances waned. She lost once to *Columbia* before MacNamara was dropped. Then *Columbia* and *Easterner* were eliminated, and thereafter *Weatherly* scored three straight wins over *Nefertiti* in zephyrs that never reached eight knots.

AMERICA'S CUP—1964
"Tack"

*In the second race of an uninspired series, in twenty knots of breeze
and under overcast skies, Bavier started* Constellation *about four
boatlengths to leeward of Sovereign. Both boats sailed equally until
they ran into the spectator wakes to the west of the course.
Sovereign tacked first, and on the starboard tack ran almost directly
into a heavy swell, which caused her to slam and hobby-horse.
Bavier, tacking behind Sovereign, did not attempt to squeeze above
her, but drove off through the swell and through Sovereign's lee.
Sovereign, laboring, made excessive leeway.*

52

On August 25, the Selection Committee made an easy decision and selected *Weatherly* and Mosbacher for the second defense in the Twelves.

Sir Frank Packer was the first of a series of challengers to fall into his own formula for defeat. He was an individual, not a syndicate, and therefore had a sort of built-in obligation to omniscience and an inclination to back his own mistakes in judgment. He was a man whose success resulted from strong moves at the right time, and a man who delegated work and harried the workers until the job was done to his satisfaction. He crystallized in his mind a formula for success, and was willing to apply it to this new field.

Match racing in twelve meters is not a business technique, it is an art form. A relaxed skipper like Bill Ficker or an intense one like Corny Shields can each be magnificent, and as different as Picasso from Wyeth. But each must find his own means of expression and extend it to his opponent. Match racing starts with perfection of technique, progresses to sensitivity to stimulus, and arrives at perfection of response. The ideal helmsman has a lot of the computer in him, but the savor of his product comes from a salting of Svengali. Mosbacher is famous for living in an opponent's mind and putting the hex on him. Mosbacher's opponent does what Mosbacher wants him to do unless he is wholly his own man.

Sir Frank Packer was born rich and died richer. He built a publication empire of papers and magazines and T.V. and radio stations which was known appropriately to his dominated employees as "Packerstan." With characteristic brilliance, he managed to pry unprecedented concessions from the New York Yacht Club, and to employ the painstaking and thorough Alan Payne as his designer.

Payne had observed the 1958 races and had been at the Ida Lewis press conference when Bill Wallace of the *New York Times* asked Harry Sears, "Commodore, now that you have the fastest twelve meter in the world, would you build another if there were another challenge?" Sears turned to Olin Stephens and said, "That would depend on whether Olin could design a faster one." With a self-deprecating smile, Olin replied, "I already have."

Payne knew he was lucky to be sailing against *Weatherly*, but he had a massive task nevertheless, and he performed magnificently. His sails were excellent, his boat was superior to *Weatherly*, and he had a crew that might have been superior also had they been permitted to learn their intricate ballet together.

But Packer was running things. He refused to choose his crew and his skipper and let them develop flawless routines, subconscious relationships, and total, responsible independence. Instead, he hired the elderly *Gleam* as a trial horse, and put his crew through drills until they responded with the mute obedience of Yo-Yos. (Besides, beating a trial horse has about as much value in training for an America's Cup race as beating your wife does in preparation for a bout with Muhammad Ali.) Skipper Jock Sturrock might have developed beyond a crude tactician and a rough and ready helmsman, but he was never given total responsibility. Moreover,

Packer changed two men on the crew lineup the morning of the first Cup race, and put the inexperienced navigator Magnus Halvorsen on board in place of Terry Hammond, who had by that time become thoroughly familiar with the vagaries of local Rhode Island waters.

Mosbacher knew he had a slower boat, and that the series could turn into a replay of *Vim*–*Columbia* if Sturrock ever got the clue. If the press was not already aware of the situation, they became aware in the first race, and nervously maintained a conspiracy of silence by mutual agreement.

The day before the race, both skippers were trying to psych each other out via the press. Mosbacher's "The start is 50 percent of the battle between matched boats," meant that Sturrock had better give up if he lost the start. Sturrock's "Our only match racing at home is the Melbourne Challenge Cup, and that isn't elaborate—we don't practice at all, we just ring each other up and have a bash of an afternoon," meant that the Australians were casual and likely to do the unexpected.

AMERICA'S CUP—1964
"Around the Cup Buoy"
At the end of the third leg in race two, Constellation *grinds in her*
sheets for another weather leg. Peter Scott's crew carries
Sovereign's *spinnaker to the last second, and then drags it down in*
the genoa's backwind.

56

There was an exceptional crowd on September 15, so many and so badly controlled by the Coast Guard that the start had to be postponed. Spectators actually sailed between the boats and to windward of *Gretel,* and Sturrock could no more get away from Mosbacher than a pool ball can get away from the cushions. Some socially conscious news-media personnel had written about the Coast Guard's wasting taxpayers' money patrolling for the private New York Yacht Club, so the Coast Guard nervously left a lot of boats home, wasting the same costs in idleness.

The initial course was a twenty-four-miler—twice around a windward-leeward course, six miles on a leg. This course is really dangerous to a defense, because it gives a good downwind boat a last leg advantage. After this series, the NYYC realized its peril and made all the races "Olympic course," ending on a windward leg. However, the first race was easily to *Weatherly* because Sturrock didn't know his boat, and didn't realize the extent to which the spectator fleet would box him in.

Sturrock got a good start in the initial race in safe leeward position with free air. He went off south for fifteen minutes, footing well, and then ran into the massive spectator fleet, which forced him to tack back to Mosbacher, who was on starboard. Sturrock dipped under Mosbacher's stern, and Mosbacher, below Sturrock, tacked and slowly squeezed up under him, forcing him to pinch and lose speed. Sturrock tacked back toward the spectators and the bobble. At this point the wind shifted, letting Mosbacher up to the mark, and Sturrock's navigator held him on a losing tack for two minutes, waiting for the wind to shift back, sailing away from Mosbacher and the mark. This fatal tactic cost at least the time it took, and Sturrock rounded 1:43 back.

Gretel went nicely down the next leg, gaining, and rounded only 1:08 back. Then the entire operation degenerated. The wind picked up to twenty-five, and Mosbacher, leading, set a smaller genoa. Sturrock set a bigger genoa in a desperation tactic, and dropped back to 3:57. Eventually, in what became a procession, Weatherly won by 3:43.

Like the first round of a boxing match, the

first match race tells you for the first time how you compare with your opponent. Mosbacher found that *Gretel* could outfoot him to windward if she wasn't squeezed up to weather, and that she was faster than *Weatherly* directly downwind, as she had gained on both spinnaker legs. Sturrock found that he couldn't point with *Weatherly,* the way *Gretel* was presently set up. *Weatherly,* with Hood aboard, had been sailing on her genoas and luffing her main, thus standing higher and flatter than *Gretel.* Sturrock drove off full, and found *Gretel* tender. Wiser heads got to Sturrock during the night, and he gave up his initial plan to add ballast, and instead hardened the headstay and sailed higher.

The pattern of defeat emerges. The first Cup race is very late to be learning your boat—but how can you learn if there's no competition with reality? Also, the spectator fleet made good competition impossible. Packer decreed that *Gretel* would ask for a layday after every race, mainly to wear out the spectators, but also to practice the lessons learned in the actual race. This is the sort of practice from good evidence that *Weatherly* had enjoyed for the previous three months, and that every American contender has before the races start. Now, during the layday, Sturrock found that he did not have an overtender boat; instead he found that she could be tuned to go very well to windward, with a bar-taut headstay and a well-stretched jib. A good many of *Gretel's* sails were Hood sails, and Ted has been known to murmur, sotto voce, "It's really hard to get it too tight." What some reporters had characterized as "a heavy-weather crew on a light-weather boat" had been sorted a little.

Gretel won the next race. They didn't plan it that way, but had winning thrust upon them. Packer threw Halvorsen off as navigator, but instead of using Hammond, he put in Archie Robertson (looking for a quick learner?). *Gretel* wore a *Vim* mainsail (1958), in a breeze that was eighteen–twenty knots from the southwest at the start and developed gusts to thirty. Sturrock entirely avoided Mosbacher and did a timed start, crossing the line downwind at the committee boat, spinning, breaking out his genoa, and going for the line. So did Mosbacher, a hair

AMERICA'S CUP—1964
"Around the Weather Mark"
Collection of Mr. and Mrs. William Boyd, Jr.
*In lighter air and under brighter skies, Constellation rounds the
first mark in the third race with a good lead, and reaches off for
the wing mark. A solid Navy tug provides an excellent radar target
for the committee boat and a highly visible object for both navigators.*

later, and Sturrock crossed one length ahead and to windward. *Gretel* was now sailing as stiff and as high as *Weatherly*, but with *Weatherly* to leeward, she was not quite as fast, and in nine minutes Mosbacher had a safe leeward berth.

Gretel now initiated a tacking duel. She had unique cross-linked coffee-grinders, and with four men on the handles against two of "Mosbacher's midgets" (the Aussies were massive), *Gretel* tacked faster and gained steadily for ten tacks, when *Weatherly* split tacks. When *Weatherly* came back, she crossed four boatlengths ahead.

This episode showed Mosbacher an advantage that he would use for the rest of the series. Sturrock could bring his boat rapidly to maximum speed when he had *Weatherly* on a parallel course to check against, but he didn't know *Gretel*'s trim well enough to achieve maximum performance without a yardstick. With Mosbacher ahead, *Gretel* got bad advice from her navigator and tacked too short for the mark. Mosbacher laid it, and *Gretel* had to pinch around. She rounded, however, only twelve sec-

onds behind *Weatherly*, having gained two boatlengths on *Weatherly* in the last eight minutes of the leg.

The course for the second race was a triangular course, so the second leg was a reaching leg. I was broadcasting the race, and commented on my astonishment that *Gretel*, whose reaching had been tank-predicted to be her most powerful point of sail, was merely steering above *Weatherly*'s course and doing nothing with vang or sheet experimentation to improve her speed. Sailing a slightly longer course than Mosbacher in a wind that made sailing angle irrelevant did not seem like a sound tactic. As a result, *Gretel* lost two seconds on this processional leg, and reached the second mark fourteen seconds (two boatlengths) back, with her pole ready for a spinnaker reach. *Gretel* lost the first leg, but the tables were soon to turn.

Weatherly had her Hood spinnaker drawing as *Gretel* set her Hood spinnaker. Mosbacher immediately felt the effect of *Gretel*'s windshadow, and, too late, started to luff up in search of clear air. As his pole went forward, his spinnaker collapsed, filled explosively, parted the afterguy, and slammed the pole against the headstay. The pole bent; the spinnaker dragged water. Sturrock, used to surfing in Australia's strong winds, had paid *Gretel* off perfectly on a single great wave face that roared up out of nowhere, caught it, and surfed for two hundred yards past the helpless *Weatherly*, past any tactical control that Mosbacher could lay on him, and into a commanding lead. It took the shocked *Weatherly* six minutes to get a new pole up and a spinnaker drawing. *Gretel* set a course record, and won by forty-seven seconds.

There was an epic celebration that night. The Aussies had adopted a grundgy little bar called "The Cameo" as their pub and had altered the sign in the window to "The Royal Cameo Yacht Squadron." The roaring night after the great victory made it Newport's hot spot, and at the end of the season the owners sold it and retired to Florida.

Other reactions to the victory were varied. Bus Mosbacher invited me over for a drink, met me at the door, took me into a private room and told me in firm terms that I was a reporter, not a tactical adviser, and that my comments on the radio were to be limited to what was happening and what had happened, not what he or Sturrock might do.

"This is the biggest poker game in the world," he said, "and if he ever gets the notion that he can beat us on any point of sailing, he might just sail off by himself and do it." Then I got the drink.

Good, careful Alan Payne had been worried about the reaching leg, too, and he widened the mainsheet horse to give *Gretel* a better reaching lead. The wind, during the layday for which the Australians had unfortunately asked, blew at thirty-two knots, and the Americans went out and practiced spinnaker sets and jibes.

The third race was a terrible anticlimax. The air was very light and it gave *Gretel* a whole new set of problems and no clues. Sturrock did not use the 1958 Hood *Vim* mainsail, but for the light air set a full Tasker main which looked soggy at the head. Sturrock did a magnificent timed start with the gun; Mosbacher crossed

63

AMERICA'S CUP—1964
"Finish"

Cut to ribbons by spectator wakes, the sea reflects hazy cumulus
clouds as Sovereign drives toward the finish. Constellation,
hearing the gun, stands up to await her rival. The spectators,
well-behaved until the outcome is obvious, have gunned ahead to
wait at the finish line. The Committee boat rolls violently beam on to
their wakes.

64

twelve seconds later and to leeward. *Weatherly* was not about to let *Gretel* march away full-and-by. As Mosbacher began squeezing up toward *Gretel*, Sturrock initiated a tacking duel. Twenty-two tacks later, both boats were even, and *Weatherly* refused to respond to Sturrock's final tack in the series.

Without *Weatherly* as a yardstick, and with a new mainsail which required all new trim points, *Gretel* simply dropped back for the remainder of the leg, rounding fifty-eight seconds back. In the next downwind leg, Mosbacher ignored Sturrock and sailed directly for the bottom mark. Sturrock reached back and forth in an effort to generate boat speed, and ran into the spectator fleet before each jibe. This tactic was hopelessly wrong, and *Gretel* went around the bottom mark in very light air some twenty-four minutes behind. Then, sailing the boat directly and with no attempt at tactics, Sturrock closed to sixteen minutes, and on the final downwind leg, to 8:40. Plainly, the Aussies lost the second race because they didn't know where their boat's competitive point was. Learning by doing in the third race is

expensive, but the race should have said loud and clear to Sturrock: Play it straight, mate.

The third race confirmed a glaring weakness in the Aussies' ability to move their own boat without a competitive yardstick, but it also showed that when they did find the tune, *Gretel* was faster downwind and to weather than *Weatherly* even in light air. And it told Mosbacher that Sturrock tended to rush to desperation measures in clutch situations. Mosbacher carefully noted all these things.

In the fourth race, *Gretel* came to the line with a new, rather full, Hood mainsail, and a new Hood 3.5 genoa with a zippered luff. The wind puffed gently from the southwest at four to ten knots. The race was three legs, windward, reaching, and leeward. Following his pattern, Mosbacher got a safe leeward start on Sturrock's timed start, crossing the line a little ahead where he could hold Sturrock high and kill *Gretel's* speed advantage. Sturrock couldn't seem to get his new Hood 3.5 genoa tuned, and shifted to a Rolly Tasker four-ounce, which lost shape, and finally to an effective *Vim* Hood, thus raising the question: Can a crew of valiant learners learn to trim three jibs on one leg of the course?

Once the jib question was settled, Sturrock tried a tacking duel, but this time the Long Island Sound Fox had an answer. Each time *Gretel* tacked, *Weatherly* held on for a minute and tacked. With no yardstick, Sturrock would run for that minute at less than speed. Mosbacher was thus able to neutralize any advantage Sturrock might have gained in a tacking duel. After twenty tacks, *Weatherly*'s navigator accurately predicted a slight windshift, and *Weatherly* simply abandoned the tacking duel and headed straight for the next mark, rounding at a comfortable 1:26 ahead of *Gretel.*

The second leg, reaching, found Sturrock on his own and doing well. It was a straight procession, and *Gretel* took back thirty-one seconds, to round fifty-five seconds back with only the square run to go. Mosbacher's set was difficult; he found himself in a bobble of spectator wakes from the fleet which, at the last minute, ran ahead of him and then parked above the mark. *Gretel* arrived in smoother water, set quickly and

flawlessly, and was probably only forty-five seconds back as her bag started to draw. The wind had picked up to sixteen knots, and *Gretel* began to make little runs on wave faces, visibly closing the gap on *Weatherly.* Jubilation reigned among Australian reporters on the press boat, for at this pace *Gretel* could obviously overtake *Weatherly* well before the finish.

But Mosbacher was a student of history as well as performance, and he used the trick with which Sherman Hoyt had twice robbed Sopwith and *Endeavour* of certain victory. He sharpened to a reach away from the finish and set a genoa. At first, Sturrock hoisted his genoa inside his spinnaker and accelerated, eating away at Mosbacher's lead at almost a third better speed. For two minutes he was actually closer to the finish line than *Weatherly,* but he sharpened still more onto Mosbacher's course, took down his spinnaker, and dropped speed. Mosbacher gauged his move exactly, set spinnaker, dropped genoa and ran for the mark. The wind had faded back to ten knots, and Sturrock went back to spinnaker and chased Mosbacher. But Mosbacher's play for

AMERICA'S CUP—1967
"Syndicate Mates"
With Rudi Schaefer's America *and Bob Douglas's* Shenandoah *to
leeward, where educated spectators belong,* Intrepid *practices on a
pleasant June afternoon with her syndicate partner* Constellation.
Intrepid's *fuller ends and longer waterline give her a look of
increased power;* Constellation's *fully developed sails and her flexed
mast show her ultimate tune.*

68

time had worked, and now there was not enough space left to close the gap. The wind was down to eight when *Weatherly* crossed the line, twenty-six seconds ahead of *Gretel* in the closest finish yet in an America's Cup contest. Steadily gaining in the final minutes, *Gretel* would have won on a course a hundred yards longer.

The Aussies asked for a layday. "We keep asking for laydays," they said, "because we have a lot to learn, and we need every hour we can get. And we've reached the point where we're picking it up rather fast." When Mosbacher was asked, "Were you worried?" he replied, "Are you kidding? I'm going home to bed!"

The press was puzzled. Quite plainly, *Gretel* could have won the race by using known quantities in the starting leg, and by simply staying with a good thing on the final stretch. Who had made the decisions? Why? It is hard to believe that a well-coached schoolboy would have let Mosbacher get away with that downwind shuffle, or that an Olympic medalist, which Sturrock was, would have bought it.

The last race in the 1962 series saw Mosbacher at his cool best. His start was a masterpiece. He forced *Gretel* over the line, dipped the line, and started in the safe leeward position on starboard tack. He held on, ahead and to leeward, for seventeen minutes. *Gretel* tacked away, came back, but could not quite cross *Weatherly*. Sturrock then initiated a tacking duel, but, as described by Geoffrey Spranger in the Newport *Daily News,* Mosbacher now had his defense well organized.

The reason for *Weatherly's* tactic was soon evident, for each time Sturrock tacked, *Weatherly* would continue on, and, as Sturrock came back on the other board, *Weatherly* would tack away from him. As a result, *Weatherly,* which gets settled to sailing faster than *Gretel,* never let *Gretel* hasten her tacks until *Weatherly* was moving strongly. In the lumpy sea, it became apparent that *Gretel* couldn't get adjusted and moving as soon after tacking as *Weatherly,* and so the Mosbacher maneuver was successful. *Gretel* tacked faster but she didn't sail as well just after tacking, and Mosbacher was making her sail after tacking. The short tack problem had been solved in *Weatherly's* favor. *Weatherly* took her last tack and laid off, unable to make the mark, as

Sturrock took his ninth tack. It could have been the frightful luck that Gretel has had, or the uncanny instinct that Mosbacher *has*, but the wind obligingly moved 15 degrees to the south and let northbound *Weatherly* up to the mark. *Gretel*, headed, tacked, after she had overstood about 60 seconds worth.

What Jeff Spranger is not giving away in this article is the fact that Mosbacher knew the wind's phases off Newport, knew that the wind lifts and veers in a pattern which can be timed and recorded. Given the right velocity and the right temperature, one can call these minor wind shifts almost to the minute, and the boat that tacks in anticipation of them profits hugely over a boat that doesn't. As of 1976, no challenger for the America's Cup has profited by this pattern intentionally, and in *all* the reports of *all* the races in the era of the Twelves, no defender has been on the wrong side of a windshift when the wind was in the southwest.

The second leg, downwind, was badly handled, too. *Gretel* spent it changing spinnakers instead of sailing. She went from a white to a red, white, and blue, to a Joe Pierce bubble—to

round 2:28 back—some six hundred yards.

This six-hundred-yard lead nearly proved to be Mosbacher's undoing. Turning the corner alone and without the temptation of Mosbacher to divert him, Sturrock went to work on the boat. He hardened his backstay mercilessly, let the runners forward to flatten the lower draft of the main, and got *Gretel* rocketing along in the ten-knot air. He gained two hundred yards in half a mile and, although he was to leeward of Mosbacher, both boats were being let up toward the mark. Again, Mosbacher reached out and deflated *Gretel*. Although he must have been very close to laying the mark where he was, Mosbacher did a slow, deliberate swinging tack, and sailed off at right angles to the mark. Sturrock stood the tension for a minute more of romping toward victory, and then tacked. He never got retuned and arrived at the final windward mark 3:40 back. With slacked sheets both boats set Hood spinnakers and made a straight run for the finish line of the race and the series, finishing 3:40 apart.

The epitaph of this most closely matched of all

AMERICA'S CUP—1967
"Intrepid *and* Dame Pattie"
Collection of Hon. and Mrs. Emil Mosbacher, Jr.
In flawless weather, Intrepid, *in safe leeward position, leads* Dame
Pattie *just after a start. Average winds and clear skies were the rule*
for the 1967 series. After the first race, Coast Guard regulations
kept spectators at least a half-mile off the course, dim in the distance.

72

the America's Cup Series was beautifully written by Jeff Spranger:

In retrospect, the last two races were the same, except for the time difference. An icily accurate Mosbacher had held to his course and his decisions, and had made *Gretel* and Sturrock sail *Weatherly's* race. They were his waters, in every sense of the word, and with the knife edge of his calculation, he had cut a winning slice of the cake. He had been surprised once, but thereafter he was never surprised and never faltered.

Chapter Three
1964: *Constellation—Sovereign*

Sir Frank Packer's 1962 challenge with *Gretel* and Jock Sturrock had given a great thrust to the America's Cup scene. The challenger had been given more than an even break, and could have won the Cup with enlightened and accomplished handling. The Australian designer Payne had come up with a better and faster boat than the American retread *Weatherly*. But *Gretel* had been tank-tested in the United States, her sails were of substantially American design, and all her sailcloth was American-made, as was most of the sailcloth in the world at that time. The winches on both *Gretel* and *Weatherly* were American-made Barients. The Australian, British, and French observers who were in Newport for most of the summer of 1962 were excited by the possibilities *Gretel* suggested, and the Cup appeared to be in for some vigorous competition.

The very range of the oncoming threat, with challengers looking the ground over four years ahead of their challenges, had an aura of hijack about it. Serious meetings were held in New York, at which the NYYC laid down strong new limitations for interpreting the rules of Cup

AMERICA'S CUP—1967
"Hazy Day—Tactical Start"
On opposite tacks, Intrepid *and* Dame Pattie *sheet home for start.*
Flags on foreward mast of Committee Boat Gray Mist *indicate*
bearing of first mark; yellow flag and America's Cup buoy indicate
starting line; and red cylinder, hoisted, indicates starting gun has
been fired. Intrepid *is headed west,* Pattie *is tacking on line to lure*
Mosbacher south, away from favoring lifts. Coast Guard ships, in
background, show their new identifying stripes.

76

competition. Now the design, including testing, had to be from the country of origin. All major equipment, including sails, had to be manufactured there. These regulations moved the challenges from any other country back a few squares, but the New York Yacht Club was not through.

Previous races had been sailed over a changing course—one day a twice-around windward-leeward course, and the next day a triangle. Both courses had the built-in danger of a final leeward leg. In a leeward leg, a close-trailing boat is the tactical commander. If she's close enough to lay her windshadow on the yacht ahead, the leader must dodge and jibe to avoid being slowed and passed. On the other hand, when the final leg is to windward the leader is in tactical control and defense is a bit more certain. Therefore, beginning in 1964, all races would be sailed on the Olympic pattern: three legs to windward, with two reaching legs between the first and second windward legs, and then a square run before the final thrash to the finish line. This course puts a premium on windward ability, and a yacht who

is overtaken downwind because of a giant wave or a surfing run has a whole weather leg to recover her grace.

The NYYC, having tendered the bait of equality in the *Gretel* races, pulled it back into the mouth of the trap. The "trap" is the American selection process. Until he has the same summer-long selection drills, no challenger will ever be as well-tuned, as certain of his boat and her sails, or as knowledgeable about the subtleties of Newport weather as the home team. And prior to 1977, no challenger has had that selection period.

The summer of 1967 demonstrated that the selection process itself can be manipulated. The near miss of *Gretel* against an old boat stimulated new boats. Hood redesigned *Nefertiti* for Ross Anderson, and also took her helm, inducing in himself a renewed attack of America's Cup fever. Walter Gubelmann and Eric Ridder, sailing companions on Gubelmann's *Windigo*s for the previous ten years, formed a syndicate, with Gubelmann managing and Ridder as skipper. They managed to bring in virtually the whole list of previous syndicate members: Jack Astor, Briggs Cunningham, Gil Verney, Tom Clagett, Jack Dorrance, Roger Firestone, Avard Fuller, Frank Kellog, Charles Payson, Rudi Schaefer, Mike Vanderbilt, George Moffett, and, later, others. They built *Constellation,* probably the "better" boat that Olin Stephens had "already" designed during the summer *Columbia* was working up to championship form. Meanwhile, Pete duPont had gone to Al Luders and turned him loose on the America's Cup path to design the ultimate boat. He may have done just that.

American Eagle, as the Luders–duPont Twelve was christened, was a fairly radical departure from the conservative norm. She had virtually the same new keel shape as *Constellation,* a "fastback" transom that rounded off from several feet forward on the deck, thereby getting a measurement advantage and saving weight, and "Mount Luders"—a mound where her mast passed through the deck, which gave her a few more inches of mast height. (The height of the mast is measured "above the deck" and limited by the rule.) She had Hood sails.

Constellation was, in her time, a breakthrough boat. She had not only a "bendy" boom, but a "bendy" mast, linked coffee-grinders, a chute in the forepeak and a hole for headsails to pop through at the headstay. Aluminum and Dacron bins high inside her hull and out by the gunwales carried the sails not being used high to weather. Her cabin sole was made of almost weightless aircraft honeycomb material. Streamlined rod rigging cut wind resistance, and halyard winches below decks lowered her crew and her center of gravity. She had two complete suits of sails— Hoods and Hards.

Hard got into computer design at an early date, and Wally Ross, the president, was a frequent member of *Windigo's* afterguard. The use of the computer appealed to Gubelmann and Ridder. Gubelmann's father invented the punch-card machine and, with Thomas Watson, Sr., of NCR, founded IBM. Ridder's father owned the *Journal of Commerce.* Both younger men were thoroughly steeped in the techniques of the business world, and they set about winning the selection for the America's Cup defense

AMERICA'S CUP—1967
"Wing Mark"
With a light breeze on the surface and the promise of more aloft,
Intrepid has completed her jibe around the yard tug at the wing
mark. Her bow-man at the shrouds calls trim as she sharpens on new
reach. Dame Pattie's spinnaker softens as she runs off toward jibe at
mark. Member's yachts Melantho and Exact fly syndicate flags
above Intrepid's bow.

in a businesslike way by getting all the information they could about their own boat and telling their rivals for selection as little as possible.

Ridder, at the helm of *Constellation*, had been a world-class helmsman on *Goose*. He was pitted against Bill Cox, North American sailing champion and a meticulous statistician, on *American Eagle*, and Ted Hood on *Nefertiti*. Bob Bavier, editor of *Yachting* and son of a famous yachtsman, was alternate helmsman on *Constellation*. While Bavier was not known to have exceptional ability to move a boat, he had a reputation for using very aggressive tactics.

Cox, a great helmsman, is sensitive to the boat's tune to a remarkable degree. Sailing with him in a Fastnet Race on Bill Snaith's *Figaro* was an education in sensitivity. For a half hour he called for minor adjustments in sail trim, and for a half hour we slowly improved our speed and left the competition behind. He steered with his fingertips on the wheel, and his rather slight body was tense as a tuning fork in total concentration. Cox's weakness was this very intensity of concentration: his sensitivity to the boat was so singleminded that tactical considerations were disrupting and exhausting. In the course of the summer of 1964 he went from thin to gaunt, racing by day and painstakingly examining statistics by night. As far as I know, Cox did not have a "caller"—a tactician who watches the competition and makes the suggestions the helmsman usually follows.

One feature of the development of the Twelves to highly tuned machines is the increasing difficulty of steering them. A boat is more obedient to her helm as her rudder is larger and as it moves farther aft. However, the rudder is also a brake, and a bigger rudder is a bigger brake. Any use of the rudder puts drag on the boat's forward speed. The new keel shape on the 1964 boats had positive lift, so the 1964 boats, with the exception of *Nefertiti*, needed less lateral plane in the keel. Their rudders were minimal in size and still at the backside of the keel, well under the boat. The trim-tab, the cross-flow fence (known as the "kicker"), and the vestigial rudder that increased the waterline without increasing the measurement-according-to-rule were waiting for the 1967 generation of Twelves. The knuckle bow was beginning to appear. It increased the active waterline while diminishing the measured waterline; as the boat changed speed· this variation in the length of the waterline increased the difficulty of sensing exact trim from the steering qualities of the boat, and made the helmsman's work very wearing. George O'Day, caller for Mosbacher and himself a world-class helmsman and Olympic gold medalist, said of the spectator fleet's proximity to the *Gretel–Weatherly* races: "It's hard enough to sail these boats, without having to fight the unpredictable wakes of 50 or 100 other craft."

A Twelve is the lightest boat that can be built within "Lloyd's specifications for scantlings" with as much ballast as will float her to her required lines. She weighs in the neighborhood of thirty tons, and carries about twenty tons of lead some ten feet below water. Because of this weight, a Twelve has great momentum, and in light air at a starting line she can come head to wind and move inexorably for several minutes. Sailed with full pressure on her eighteen hundred square feet of sails (which can develop up to five pounds per square foot of pressure), she moves easily into the ten-knot speed range, and can actually be brought close to a luff without perceptible loss of speed.

The "looping" helmsman does just that. As the boat approaches maximum speed, she brings her apparent wind forward and approaches a luff. Her sheets are benchmarked, and the best trim for any given condition has been worked out over the summer, so that in a race only vestigial trimming is required. The looping helmsman rides ahead to the edge of the luff, falls off a bit or trims a bit harder, and watches his hundredth of a knot speedo. As soon as it registers a minus instead of a plus, he falls off and regains speed, and then squeezes up to weather again to maintain windward advantage. In light air, his track on the sea face is a series of gentle arcs, rarely more than three degrees either way.

The "grooving" helmsman rides off the wind a little more initially, until he gets the feel of the boat, and then gently brings her as close as possible to the wind, fine-tuning as he comes.

AMERICA'S CUP—1967

"Windward Mark"

On starboard tack with spinnaker ready, Intrepid rounds Navy tug at weather mark. She'll set spinnaker as jib drops, and then jibe onto course for square run. Dame Pattie, more than a minute back, has her spinnaker pole to port and will jibe before setting.

When he finds her track he stays there, giving trim instructions and avoiding the rudder as much as possible. To a dinghy sailor, used to instant response, or to a helmsman accustomed to the brutal power of a large ocean racer, a Twelve's vestigial steering seems about as immediate and responsive as a rowboat half-full of water.

Developing a Twelve to her full potential is a protracted battle against complex variables for the last one-tenth of 1 percent of speed. Sailing the boat back and forth by the hour, the skipper finds the exact trim for the best speed of a given sail, and even finds which of, say, three No. 1 genoas is fastest highest to windward. Every boatowner, having done his drill conscientiously, then has the sailmaker come aboard and change the shape of the new sail a little to get better speed out of it. Start, like *Constellation*, with two sailmakers and two suits of sails, add a new crew to a new boat with unique design qualities, put the whole lot on a boat where thirty tons of deadweight is punching into a sea at ten knots with an average load of four tons on the

sailcloth, which has residual stretch. Then let the sailmaker do minor recutting and stitching almost every night. After a month of this, you're still a long way from home plate. This situation Ridder and Cox faced.

Other contenders for the defense were helmsman Briggs Cunningham and sailmaker North on Pat Dougan's *Columbia*, Ted Hood on *Nefertiti*, and "coveys of Hoveys" on *Easterner*. *Easterner* had added little new gear since 1962; *Nefertiti*'s sails were well-developed; *Columbia* had been extensively improved and successfully raced on the West Coast. Against such known quantities and each other, the two new boats, *Constellation* and *Eagle*, raced and worked up their sail inventory.

An external consideration distorted the competition between *Constellation* and *Eagle*; the British challenge was an empty one. Despite extensive testing in the Davidson tank prior to 1964, the Boyd hull was not "in the ball park" and the information leaked. Also built into the British effort were all the drawbacks of both the "Packerstan" and the "establishment" approaches. Tony Boyden was a self-made thirty-five-year-old roaring boy, entirely innocent of sailing experience at any level of competition, and socially pleased to be representing The Royal Thames Yacht Club. It wasn't The Squadron, of course, but it was London.

Boyden chose for his crew a group of football players, in the naive belief that dedicated athletes could adapt to, and acquire, sailing skills through rigorous drill. His helmsman was Peter Scott, a famous sporting painter, author, conservationist, and dinghy medalist. Scott had never had a competitive season in a boat remotely comparable to a Twelve. He had a navigator, no caller, and Bruce Banks as a sailmaker. Banks had not made sails this size, and was working under the new requirement that the cloth he used be woven in "the country of origin." He had been previously expert with American cloth, but was now forced to shift to his rival Ratsey's "Vectis."

The Royal Thames knew that they could not bring *Sovereign* to a competitive level without some experience at competition. In the person of Owen Aisher, they managed to persuade millionaire Australian sheep-ranchers Frank and John Livingstone, who were then living in England, to back a second Twelve. The boat would be managed by a committee from the Royal Thames headed by Aisher. The skipper was Col. R.S.G. (Stug) Perry, who had sailed with Aisher in mid-class ocean racers. Perry had little practical experience in sail development and none in match racing. Nevertheless, *Kurrewa V* was launched in the spring of 1964, and did fairly well against *Sovereign* in the early trials. From the outset the sails for both boats were disastrous. They seemed adequate in light air, but stretched into ungainly lunchbags as it blew up.

Under the circumstances, it was apparent that the only boats a defender had to beat were the American contenders, and the situation created an unusual range of tactics. The first sign that the summer would not be an unbroken effort toward decorous perfection came when Newport blossomed with bumper stickers urging "Beat the Bird." Shortly thereafter, those using the compulsory toilet on *Constellation* found every third

AMERICA'S CUP—1967
"Beat for the Mark"
Using "Virginia Reel" cover, Intrepid, a half-mile from the mark,
gets a knock as Dame Pattie is lifted. Lift will ease Pattie clear of
spectator wakes which forced Intrepid to tack. Pattie's sails, first
from Australian cloth, have hard spot near battens.

88

sheet of paper on an entire roll rubberstamped, "Prevent Constipation." [Rules again: *Constellation*'s toilet was nonfunctional during races, as the inlet and outlet apertures were flush-sealed inside and hand-polished to a mirror finish outside. The seals were rumored to have cost about $350 each to make.]

Despite free spending for extra masts, double suits of sails, flush closures, bendy booms, and the like, *Constellation* seemed to lose with whimsical deliberation. As soon as she was going well, she would change sails and lose. Once a mainsail was worked into a smooth set, she'd fly another the next day and start recutting that. Ridder was constantly attacked by the press and there were rumbles of discontent from his crew and vigorous criticism from syndicate members. His tactics were too little and too late, his boatspeed was intermittent.

It is difficult to believe that he could do no better. Twelves may be hard to steer, but Ridder is a superior helmsman. His present all-out ocean racer, *Tempest*, has done exceptionally well. Perhaps there was plan in his apparent madness.

90

"I am but mad nor-norwest, and can tell a hawk from a handsaw!" Assume Ridder's intention was to have *Constellation* selected, and that the *Eagle*–Cox combination was, from the beginning, able to beat *Constellation*–Ridder. In the long struggle to maximize performance, one can only tune against an equivalent boat, and *Nefertiti*, *Columbia*, and *Easterner* were not equivalent boats. So, as *Constellation* got her sails to a tune that would beat *American Eagle*, or when *Eagle* changed sails in an effort to get her own checkout, *Constellation* would mistrim a bit, or change a sail and let *Eagle* win. Thus *Eagle* gained false confidence and Cox's judgment was confused as he won consistently. The NYYC expressed stern disapproval of the printed "humor"; it would have disapproved even more sternly of gamesmanship. Of course, anyone daring to voice such dark suspicions would be assured, with ardent protests, that such tactics would be obvious, that the syndicate wouldn't stand for it, and that the crew wouldn't go along with it.

In the early season races, *Eagle* won four, and *Constellation* two by narrower margins. In the midsummer series, *Eagle* won twelve, and *Constellation* four. *Constellation* had major troubles in the observation races because her rather tricky gear didn't always work through an entire race. Early in July she lost one flexible mast. On July 18, Bavier took over the helm from Ridder, who stayed aboard as skipper, and things began to look up for *Connie*. The trigger episode came in a race with *Nefertiti* in light air. At the start, Ridder scraped the Committee Boat, and was disqualified automatically. He sailed the race anyway, to show the Committee what *Connie* could do in light air, and only managed to beat Hood and *Nefertiti* by two seconds—a performance that did more harm than good to *Constellation*'s reputation.

Bavier made a new boat of her, and beat *Eagle* decisively in the last three races of the NYYC Cruise. After the cruise, Bavier was starting and main helmsman by syndicate decision. Rod Stephens, who had made the cruise with *Connie*, joined the crew as caller. Bavier made a hash of *Eagle* in the final races, winning by large margins. Coming from behind in the second race, Bavier ground *Eagle* down in a forty-two-tack duel, and won the final race by six full minutes. The syndicate, which had been in virtual revolt at midsummer, settled back with a sigh of relief and began saving for the next challenge.

As a result of the earlier performances of *Constellation*, *Eagle*'s final performances were slightly frantic. For no clear reason she used a different mainsail after the late-summer NYYC Cruise. Later, Cox said, "We finally went back to the mainsail we used winning all the races at the beginning of the season." Why *Eagle* ever stopped using the sail is a mystery locked deep in the minds of her afterguard. Or was it in *Constellation*'s game plan?

Unlike Milton's swain, Cox was not one to arise "and twitch his mantle blue / Tomorrow to fresh fields and pastures new." He got all the movies, stills, accounts, and statistics he could, and spent most of the winter trying to determine where he had gone wrong. His conclusion was subtle, undoubtedly true, and rather curious. There is no substitute for boat speed, and "VMG" (speed made good to weather) is the key

91

AMERICA'S CUP—1967
"Tacking Duel"
Collection of Hon. and Mrs. Emil Mosbacher, Jr.
Pattie, *having squeezed* Intrepid *up until she tacked away, comes*
around to cover her in light northwest breeze with Newport's
shoreline in the background. Pattie's sails, excellent downwind,
consistently lost shape in air over ten knots. Here her main will
flatten into an effective windward airfoil when full runner backstay
tension bows her mast.

to victory. Bill found out, by meticulous measurement and later experimentation with *Eagle* herself, that she was *too* well balanced. The angle of attack of an airplane's wing keeps it in the air. Unless the front edge is higher than the back edge, a wing has no lift. In a sailboat, the lead-drag angle corresponds to the angle of attack, but is in the vertical rather than the horizontal plane. A keel needs to attack the water at an angle of two or three degrees above the course made good. *Eagle* was balanced out to no-weather helm, no lead-drag angle. When *Eagle*'s mast was moved back a bit, she won the world's ocean-racing championship, broke the record for the Fastnet and is still alive and competing as *War Baby*.

The 1964 races were sad spectacles. Stug Perry never got *Kurrewa V* to a competitive pitch, and *Sovereign* was selected without competitive tuning. The whole British effort appeared to be listless. I went to Owen Aisher and offered to take two or three days' worth of pictures of his sails, so that the sailmakers could attack the problem. I made it quite clear that my motives were hopeful, my work would be a voluntary contribution, and my opinion of the sails was uncomplimentary. He sniffed and hawed his appreciation, bid me a courteous goodbye, and that was that. Spranger, in the Newport *Daily News*, remarked of *Sovereign* that, despite her winning the trials and selection, he doubted she'd be competitive using a mainsail with "a hard spot extending the whole length of the sail just forward of the battens."

Nevertheless, Bavier was taking no chances. His first start against *Sovereign* was ferocious. Drifting sleepily near the starting line, he waited until Scott sailed past him in about fifteen knots of wind. Then he sheeted home, drove down on Scott, and sat on his stern until one hundred seconds before the start. Then he broke away from Scott, sailed away from the line for forty seconds, came around, and trimmed for maximum speed. Scott was too near the line, found himself with Bavier ramming along for his stern, and sheeted home for the line. As Bavier came down on *Sovereign* at the rate of knots, and *Sovereign* painfully gathered away, Bavier luffed through Scott's wind, bore off, and was long gone before *Sovereign* got up to what passed for speed.

As is standard on the first day of the America's Cup Races, the spectator fleet, plowing around in all directions and organized behind the leader only at the last minute, had created a disgusting sea full of lumps and peaks. *Sovereign* was sailed in a manner that made the worst of the sea. Out of phase with the waves, her bow would hobbyhorse some eight feet above the troughs, fall into the next crest, and rise again, with the water pouring off her decks on both sides back to the chainplates. Meanwhile, certainly not wholly because of a better hull, *Constellation* was three hundred yards ahead, sailing steadily and neatly in smoother water.

Sovereign demonstrated her unreadiness by using three jibs in the three weather legs. As usual, *Constellation* was on the appropriate tack when the wind phased. She rounded the first mark 1:49 ahead, set a Hard spinnaker borrowed from *Eagle* when a wind shift turned the genoa reach into a run, and rounded the bottom mark

1:55 ahead. On the off-wind legs, *Sovereign* seemed to have a competitive hull, but at the end of the race, *Constellation* won by a margin of 5:34.

Bavier was much more relaxed in the second race than in the first. The wind was southwest, at twenty knots and better, and *Sovereign*'s sails had no shape. *Constellation* made a casual start without tangling at all with Scott, crossing the line abeam of Scott and at least four boatlengths to leeward. Instead of squeezing for weather advantage, Bavier gave *Constellation* a rap-full, and, still pointing seven to ten degrees higher than *Sovereign*, simply sailed above her and away. Olin Stephens later remarked dryly, "A good Twelve will make just as high to windward when she's sailed full-and-by as when she's squeezed, and go a lot faster. After all, today *Connie* was sailing as she was designed to sail." She won by 20:24.

Plainly the last two races would be meaningless. Rod Stephens stepped down as caller. K. Dun Gifford, who had been aboard as navigator early in the summer, came back on, and *Constel-*

AMERICA'S CUP—1967
"Around the Fourth Mark"
Dame Pattie, *with room to spare, bears off to a reach for mark,*
building to maximum speed. Intrepid, *around, has broken out her*
spinnaker but has not yet slowed enough to fill it. Pattie *was most*
competitive downwind, but couldn't gain enough to cover
windward deficits.

lation, using the same Hood mainsail for all the races, ended the series with two more wins over a helpless *Sovereign*. After two weak challenges some tactless reporter suggested that Britain might do better to name her next challenger *Labour Movement* and get off the tradition of empire.

Constellation's average speed for the four races was one full knot faster than *Sovereign*'s. And now, future challengers would not only have to weave their own sailcloth—they would be denied access to the Davidson towing tank that had been available to David Boyd, *Sovereign*'s designer.

The 1964 series was a classic example of how challengers lose. On the challenging side were the worst of both worlds—a self-made man arbitrarily directing his operation, supporting a boat with inadequate sails and a crew of football players. Her skipper was a small-boat champion who came to the toughest match race in the world entirely innocent of match racing. Their companion challenger *Kurrewa V* had the same sails, virtually the same hull and an adequate crew of ocean-racing types. Her skipper was remote, Olympian, and superior to the crew in the icy manner of an absentee landlord on a tour of inspection. Both managers acted like lords of the manor; both crews were drilled like troops. The challenge was in the best tradition of empire, and it lost against modern management.

One of the great strengths of the defense has been and will continue to be the skipper–crew relationship. Most American crew members own their own racing yachts; many have sailed in America's Cup matches before, have special skills (sailmaker, trimmer, tactician, navigator, yacht designer, weather expert), and are highly competitive for their positions. Once a Twelve is selected for the defense, eliminated boats immediately offer a back-up supply of fully developed sails and a reserve of highly specialized and capable crew to replace or improve the defense team. The feedback from such a crew is tremendous. A round-table conference after every practice and every trial race is routine. In the pattern of business management, the relationship between skipper and crew is similar to that between a father and an elder son, and the crew is encouraged to explore their own ideas. Yet in England, as late as 1974, when Prime Minister Heath's *Morning Cloud* was winning, his crew conference was unusual enough for a British yachting magazine to tape and publish it.

The implications of such an invidious comparison between the traditions of empire and the techniques of management may be unfair. Bad sails can certainly make all the difference, just as so subtle a thing as a perfectly balanced rig can make a fatal difference in performance. Perhaps, denied equivalent sailcloth by the change in ground rules, the challengers saw their plight as hopeless, and, like honorable gentlemen, met their loss as they were obliged to, with a stiff upper lip and traditional gallantry.

AMERICA'S CUP—1967
"Beat to the Finish"
Condemned to disappointing performance by poor sails, Dame
Pattie, *well-campaigned, lags behind* Intrepid *on the final leg of the
third race.* Intrepid, *having survived a helicopter attack and lost one
hundred yards doing it, is back in good shape and will lay the line on
the next tack.*

100

Chapter Four
A DESIGN BREAKTHROUGH
AND A STEP BACKWARDS
1967: *Intrepid—Dame Pattie*

The New York Yacht Club's defensive changes in the ground rules—ostensibly to ensure that the America's Cup contenders represent "the technology of the country of origin"—put the cat among the pigeons with a vengeance. Two Australian syndicates challenged, and, while Australia had a towing tank of sorts by this time, their sailmakers were experienced with American sailcloth. How could Australian technology achieve equivalency with American technology overnight in this vital area?

They borrowed it. Ted Hood was already sailmaker for ocean racers everywhere, and Hood International soon established looms in Australia. Sailmakers trained in Marblehead at the Hood loft were making good sails from duPont fibers woven into cloth of almost predictable characteristics. The moguls of America at the NYYC were kind to multinational American industry.

Sir Frank Packer, whose terminal infection with America's Cup fever still raged, had another answer. Since every new Cup defender was faster than her predecessor, the NYYC had,

AMERICA'S CUP—1967
"Light Air Finish—Hazy Day"
Intrepid, *perhaps the ultimate Twelve, completes her clean sweep in light airs. Her grinders, the first condemned to work a whole race below decks, emerge into the hazy sunlight to hear the celebration and cheer the losers, still three minutes and thirty-five seconds from the end of their summer's dedication to a lost cause.*

GOLINKIN

in fairness, put a grandfather clause into the rule, allowing previous challengers to use existing equipment, whatever its source. Sir Frank, who still owned *Gretel*, "repaired" her from the deck down. Careful Alan Payne was the author of the new design. This approach has the sanction of history, for legislatures have long been loath to tax the public for new Navy ships, but recognize the need for repairs. *Constitution*, which we so proudly hail in Boston, was "repaired" at least twice, and came out longer, with greater tonnage and a different hull.

Unfortunately, Sir Frank was still lord of "Packerstan," and Jock Sturrock was not about to carry Packer's weight through another challenge. Instead, he became skipper and manager for an Australian syndicate set up by retired ice cream magnate Emil Christensen and supported by fifteen commercial firms. Jan Pearce, Hood International's man in Australia, designed and trimmed the sails for Sturrock's boat, *Dame Pattie*. Packer's *Gretel* had no notable helmsman and consistent crew trouble; Sturrock, on the other hand, had a first-class crew. *Gretel* may have

been the better boat, but *Dame Pattie*'s superior management easily surmounted *Gretel*'s design advantage, and Sturrock headed for Newport.

Warwick Hood, Payne's assistant for *Gretel*, was *Dame Pattie*'s designer and had been in Newport for the 1964 *Sovereign* series. A close student of the American Twelves, the boat he produced had slightly less wetted surface than *Constellation* or *Eagle*, weighed 411 pounds more, and had virtually the same sail area. She was designed to be fast in light airs, but was no great advance from the 1964 effort.

While Payne and Hood were refining the current wisdom of twelve meters, Bill Strawbridge of Philadelphia signed Olin Stephens for the 1967 defense. Strawbridge, a friend of Pete duPont's, had been in the shore support division for *Eagle*'s effort and had contributed his own time and the use of his tender *Melantho* to *Eagle*. Infected by the America's Cup bug, he went to Jack Dorrance, Burr Bartram, Mike Vanderbilt, and Pat Haggerty and rounded up a syndicate and an initial $600,000. He later brought in several more old syndicate hands to bring his total over

$800,000 and turned Olin Stephens loose to design a breakthrough Twelve.

Since Twelve design is a continuing affair, the S & S office, whose naval and commercial business is much larger than their yachting business, set up a sort of continuing development project on Twelves to keep abreast of possibilities. Mario Tarabochia, son of an Italian yachtbuilder and a pilgrim to the S & S shrine, was the S & S Twelve thinker in the yachting division. Of course the Twelves were only part of his work, and the yachting division was abreast of all experiment and success in the yachting field. Ocean-racing development was intense: the cruiser–racer concept was giving way to the all-out racer, and a lot of experimentation was being done by a new generation of young architects, many of whom had worked and trained at S & S.

By the time the lines for the new Twelve had been tank-tested and drawn, ocean-racing experiments on trim-tabs, kickers, cavitation plates, fin keels, minimized wetted surface, inhibited cross flow, and the like had borne marketable fruit. *Intrepid,* as the new boat was named, was a departure from any Twelve before her. She had less actual keel than earlier boats, and at the end of the keel there was a vestigial rudder (a "trim-tab"), widest at its bottom instead of having the conventional half-heart shape. On either side of its hinge were spring bronze fairing strips to delimit turbulence caused by the slot between keel and rudder. From the top of this small rudder to the end of the waterline, a fin, a little over two feet deep, led back to the actual rudder. The rudder was quite small, quite thick where it rotated inside the fin, and longer at the bottom than at top. The rudder also had a fairing strip, and the combination of the two carried the hull lines out at least two feet beyond the measured waterline. The hull seemed very lean forward, and a long, sheering plane carried from the front of the waterline down in a slope to the bend of the keel. The forward body of *Intrepid,* under water, was quite full (as it had to be to float some fifty-eight thousand pounds).

The deck had as many surprises as the hull. The winches disappeared below deck or into a

AMERICA'S CUP—1967
"Old Timer's Race"
America, *her professional crew of seven aided by eight crew
members from* Intrepid, *sailed away from the larger (and heavier)*
Shenandoah. America's *original lines, tank-tested by Sparkman &
Stephens before the plans for her replica were drawn for Rudi
Schaefer, tested faster than a twelve meter. "And she was designed,"
remarked Olin Stephens, "by a genius with a jackknife!" Owner
Schaefer's love for his boat was so great that he bought a
"gollywobbler" for this race—in case* Shenandoah *got ahead. It
was never used.*

GOLINKIN

large cockpit. A pair of small wheels, one on each side of the cockpit, replaced the larger helm in the center. The boom was so low that a standing helmsman looked right at it, and the deck was more absent than present. Cut away from the deck were a hole forward for sails to emerge from, two more holes beside the mast for spinnakers to disappear into, a big cockpit hole, a tailer's hole amidships of the deck, and finally, a hole behind the helmsman so the observing "coach" could stand out of the way of the troops.* Barient designed some new below-deck coffee-grinders, and now, with cross-linking, four great apes could wind away and bring in the two-ton load on a tacked genoa with greater speed than ever before; meanwhile, they were spared both sunburn and any knowledge of what was happening to their opponent. The radical design of *Intrepid*'s deck caused ocean racers and

newspaper reporters alike to make dark prophecies about what would happen the first time she was out in heavy weather, but nothing ever did.

Lowering the boom toward the deck was, to my way of thinking, the most interesting thing about *Intrepid*. Earlier, three Sparkman & Stephens ocean racers had been built to the same underwater design—*Revenoc, White Mist,* and *Figaro III*. They once spent a day off Mystic experimenting with the area under the boom to see how it affected boat speed. *Figaro III* had a doghouse, but the others did not. Each boat carried a Dyer Dhow dinghy, with chocks which would accept the dinghy in either an upright or an inverted position. Varying their roles, they sailed alternately with the dinghy upright, turned over, or with it off in about seven knots of air to windward, and each time the boat with the upright dinghy slowly ate her way ahead, demonstrating the advantage of closing the gap between the boom and the deck.

The business of lowering the boom was a matter of great concern to the defenders, since

*An upper section of *Constellation*'s mast was superlight titanium, and she even experimented (abortively, it broke) with a carbon-boron boom.

the challenger could increase his sail area by imitating it. The situation called for a bit of gamesmanship. When the Aussies and the Americans inspected each other's boats for the first time at the official measuring, the big question was how to divert the Australians' attention from the boom. Of course, the sail would not be hoisted and the end of the boom would be held aloft by a crutch, so not much would be obvious, but still. . . .

The Americans had been very diligent in shaving off weight. They eliminated winches by using clamps which made one winch available for successive sheets, and eliminated cleats by using tugboat hitches around the winches themselves. On official measurement day, at George O'Day's suggestion, they simply took a few more winches off the deck in addition to the ones already removed. The Aussies were a bit crisp about *Intrepid* being measured winchless, so the Americans obligingly replaced *all* the winches, thus diverting attention to the winches and at the same time concealing the actual number of winches they had eliminated. Such minuscule

secrets illuminate the hairline closeness of competition.

The American trials started early, unofficially beginning with the Philip Roosevelt Memorial Trophy Races in Oyster Bay and proceeding to a series of "Observation Trials" there. With City Island's many boatyards nearby, Oyster Bay is a great location for races that result in repairs or alterations.

Intrepid, with Mosbacher as skipper, was the new boat this year, and her opposition was redoubtable in prospect. Bob McCullough, who would himself organize a syndicate and campaign *Valiant* (S & S's only goof), skippered *Constellation;* George Hinman, who has been somehow involved in every Twelve campaign, and who had been the bête noire of the starting line with *Weatherly,* skippered an updated *American Eagle.* Briggs Cunningham, winning skipper of *Columbia,* had the helm of *Weatherly; Columbia,* redesigned by S & S and rebuilt by Gerry Driscoll, came to the line with Bill Ficker driving. Ficker was personally unknown on the East Coast, but had won the Congressional Cup match racing

AMERICA'S CUP—1970
"Intrepid II and Valiant—Final Trials"
*The worst place from which to watch a boat race is the Committee
Boat on a gray, cold day. Only the start, two roundings of the
bottom mark, and the finish are visible. Tactics, sail changes, tactical
tours-de-force, breaks, and disasters are horizon distant or squawked
on the VHF. While the competition lasts, the committee monitors
wind changes, sends out mark boats to move the new, smaller marks
(challenges for the navigator), and records times from the "chase
boat" which chaperones all roundings. Here the Intrepid II
crewman, on the foredeck to strike sails, relieves the committee for
the day. Valiant, almost impossible to steer well, won the early
trials, but lost (as she does here) five out of six in the finals.*

series in California, and had been World Star Class champion.

Intrepid, with undeveloped sails and an absolutely superb crew, opened her campaign by winning all three of the Philip Roosevelt fleet races. In the June 5–9 observation series, she lost one race by rounding the wrong mark while she was ahead. Since *Columbia* had not yet arrived, the series was four to one for *Intrepid,* four to one for *Eagle,* two to three for *Constellation,* and 0 to 5 for *Weatherly* (who was filling in for *Columbia*). The rest of the contenders looked with respect at the new girl and went off to the yards for a face-lift before their next appearance. *Constellation* had her rear end filled out a bit and a "kicker" added. The kicker prevents cross flow from the leeward side of the hull, where the water pressed down by the hull and keel tends to break up across the water flowing directly back along the windward side, thus producing drag. It also probably stretches the laminar flow on the leeward side a little, but at the expense of additional wetted surface. Later, *Eagle* also got a kicker and a bendy boom.

The preliminary selection trials were held July 6–18. The late alterations to *Eagle* and *Constellation* didn't seem to do much good, and the surprises came from *Columbia.* On July 6, *Columbia* beat *Constellation* by fifty-seven seconds. Mosbacher, skippering *Intrepid,* was badly beaten at the start by George Hinman, but managed to drive *Intrepid* through *Eagle's* lee to win by thirty-nine seconds. The feat was the more remarkable because *Intrepid's* mainsail was still in the formative stages and looked to be overfull and luffing up to three and four feet back from the mast. The entire period was plagued by fog, and the Twelves raced only six times in thirteen days. *Columbia* and *Constellation* tied at three each, and each beat the other once. *Eagle* was zip for the lot, and *Intrepid* was unbeaten.

The New York Yacht Club Cruise was exciting. It blew hard when the fog wasn't too thick to race, and two more Twelves were added, *Nefertiti* and *Sceptre,* purchased by motion picture tycoon Eric Maxwell. Both had kickers added to their sterns, but neither managed to beat the contenders. The results of the first race were *Intrepid* by 2:34 over *Columbia, Constellation,* and *Eagle,* in that order. The second race was scored in the same sequence. The third was sailed in rough seas and strong winds—steady at twenty-five knots and gusting in the thirties. *Intrepid* and *Constellation* were both dismasted, and that was that for the New York Yacht Club Cruise.

Intrepid came back from the cruise, put in her spare mast, and went out for practice days. She had a heart-shaped "cavitation plate" at the top of her trim-tab, pointed end forward, and she changed it for a smaller one. Her rudder, already perilously small to an eye accustomed to generations of larger rudders, was changed for one still smaller. She was proving less weatherly than *Constellation,* and had to be driven off and "footed." Driven, she ate to weather satisfactorily.

These minor adjustments and fussings with tab, rudder, deck layout, position of fittings and the like went on ceaselessly until the start of the Selection Trials. A syndicate member moaned, "My God, we buy them a boat and they seem to be determined to reduce it to dust and filings!" But the real intention of the fussing and adjusting was to keep the crew at fever pitch. While *Intrepid* fussed with details, redesigned *Columbia,* sensing her superiority to other contenders, added Lowell North, sailmaker and World Star and Congressional Cup champion, to her crew, thus infecting him with America's Cup fever.

The Selection Trials started on August 16. *Intrepid* beat *Constellation* by over five minutes; *Columbia* beat *American Eagle* by over ten minutes. Jimmy the Greek offered odds that *Intrepid* would win the America's Cup by four straight, thus anticipating the Selection Committee. On the seventeenth there was no wind. On the eighteenth *Intrepid* beat *Eagle* by ten minutes, and *Columbia* beat *Constellation* by three. On the nineteenth, twentieth, twenty-first and twenty-second there was fog thick enough to cut, stack and export to London. On the twenty-second, *Intrepid* beat *Columbia* by 1:30, and *Constellation* beat *Eagle.* The Selection Committee put on their NYYC straw hats, made the launch journey to the Newport Shipyard, and thanked *Eagle* and

AMERICA'S CUP—1970
"France *and* Gretel II—*Selection Races*"
In the third race between France *and* Gretel II, *Louis Noverraz*
sharpens to avoid Gretel's windshadow. On a gray, cold, forbidding
day, France's *sails degenerated on the weather legs and*
killed her challenge.

GOLINKIN

Constellation for their efforts. Baron Bich, the French pen magnate, stood on the dock in a white yachting uniform and nodded sagely in approval of this meticulous formality.

There was no fog on the twenty-third and twenty-fourth, and *Intrepid* won, first by seven minutes, then by four minutes. On the evening of the twenty-fourth, the launch again arrived at the Newport Shipyard and The Hats congratulated Mosbacher and his crew. Syndicate member Pat Haggerty's *Beyondan* was tied opposite *Intrepid* at the dock, the champagne started flowing, and delight was everywhere. After the inexplicable unevenness of *Constellation*'s performance in the previous trials, the 1967 Syndicate's experience was pleasant indeed.

During this time, Sturrock and his crew were out every day sailing *Dame Pattie*. They went north in Narragansett Bay, set up a triangular course and worked their sail handling around the buoys until they were perfect. They sailed the America's Cup course whenever the Americas weren't using it, working on weather evaluation,

wave patterning, and sail trim for the heavier swells encountered outside the Bay. One day, shortly after *Intrepid*'s selection, the Australians encountered *Columbia* amiably sailing the course in a soft summer breeze. The two boats went to weather for about twenty minutes, neither gaining on the other, and then broke off.

New York Yacht Club officials expressed their distress at this breach of decorum. Perhaps they were reminded of a similar incident in 1851, when the schooner *America* sailed to weather against the British cutter *Laverock*. *America* sailed smartly above *Laverock*'s wake in a fresh morning breeze, and came to anchor in Cowes "a quarter, or perhaps a third of a mile ahead," thereby putting up the wind in the yachting gentry and ruining chances for a good wager.

Even though Sturrock had slipped from under Packer's thumb, he still had the insuperable handicap of any challenger: there was no genuine competition to tune against. The process of competitive refinement, sailmaker against sailmaker, skipper against skipper, crew against crew—the process of honing a crew, of importing a specialist where needed, and of profiting by the successful experiments of the defeated contenders for the defense by inheriting sails, equipment, even crew—all these were denied by the challenger in the singleness of his challenge and the remoteness of his resources. Christensen and his syndicate gave Sturrock excellent financial support and gave splendid parties for the twelve meter crowd and their guests and friends in Newport, but they were not sailors and could not offer advice or tactical assurance to their helmsman. In an undistinguished series, Sturrock made only one tactical mistake, yet he went down in four straight without ever having been competitive after the starts.

The first race went to *Intrepid* by 5:58, in a wind consistently over fifteen knots. Sturrock's game plan was to start to leeward and ahead on a timed start, to force Mosbacher to tack, then to initiate a tacking duel that would theoretically allow the challenger to eat away at the defender and consume her. The start came out well.

Sturrock hit the line a boatlength ahead of *Intrepid* and a boatlength to leeward; but squeeze up he could not. He had a twelve-ounce mainsail which was only three weeks old. It had looked quite shapely as he set it off Castle Hill for a good look, and it had held shape during the round-de-round of the starting maneuvers. But the wind came on at the start, and when Sturrock tried to squeeze *Intrepid,* his main bellied out, developed a hard spot almost its whole length, and backwinded outrageously near to the battens. Instead of giving him speed, it simply laid *Dame Pattie* over beyond her sailing lines and kept her wallowing in the wash of the spectator fleet. To make things worse, President Kennedy had come to the races aboard a destroyer accompanied by two more destroyers. As they kept pace with the lead boat during the start and for part of the first leg, the three gray cliffs created a massive confusion of the wind, particularly the wind of the following boat. After the first leg, the Commander-in-Chief lost interest and went back to Newport, taking with

AMERICA'S CUP—1970
"Starting Line"
In the first start of a controversial series, Hardy drives Gretel II *off*
for speed while Ficker squeezes Intrepid II *to weather. An increasing*
nor'easter presages heavy winds which will bag Gretel's *sails, break*
a spinnaker pole, and put her foredeck boss overboard.

him some eight hundred spectators.

A Newport *Daily News* reporter, violating the paper's normally enthusiastic stand on all matters affecting the U.S. Navy's presence in Newport, remarked,

Why anybody with an ounce of sense thinks a destroyer, let alone three, has any business within five miles of two sailing craft defies comprehension.

Whatever the reason for Sturrock's choice of a heavy-weather mainsail, it was certainly a mistake. The *Dame* had spent the summer practicing with a 7.5-ounce main, some 2.5 ounces lighter than the usual U.S. twelve meter main, and simply hadn't developed the main they chose for this stanza. Their choice of jibs also showed either indecision, ignorance, or desperation, as they set different genoas on the three windward legs, bowed the mast and the boom to the limits, and tried every adjustment possible on the main, from ragging it to hauling it to weather. Their maneuvers were to no avail, as *Intrepid* stood like a church and ate blithely to weather in clear water. The spectator fleet closed

in ahead of *Dame Pattie*, about a half-mile away on both sides, as she dropped behind, making it mandatory that her tactics conform to Mosbacher's. As the spectator wakes met before her, *Pattie* wallowed badly and finished a dismal 5:58 back.

The message wasn't all gloomy, however. She had gained time on the reaching and running legs, and was able to do so for the rest of the series. Sturrock would be okay if he could stay within striking distance—just to the first weather mark.

The second race was more competitive and more interesting. *Dame Pattie* was quite a good light-weather boat—probably, with comparable sails, as good as any American Twelve save *Intrepid*. She was generally faster than *Intrepid* downwind, where the cut of the sails is more important than the strength and predictability of the sailcloth. With her 7.5-ounce main, *Dame Pattie* moved well before the start, and Sturrock made exactly the same start for the second race as for the first, with exactly the same results. The wind was a little fluky and never got over fourteen knots, staying largely in the seven-to-ten range.

After the start *Pattie* was able to point and foot quite well, and *Intrepid* had to be driven off to make her best speed. Sturrock squeezed *Pattie* up to weather and forced *Intrepid* to tack. He initiated a tacking duel in which *Pattie* was able to hold *Intrepid,* with neither boat gaining as they made slowly toward the weather mark. As the wind fell into its "phasing" pattern, Mosbacher lagged a tack, and *Pattie* found herself on the wrong side of a wind shift, being knocked as *Intrepid* was lifted. To recover two lost boat-lengths, Sturrock tried a false tack on Mosbacher, whose caller was Vic Romagna. Romagna and Mosbacher did not respond to Sturrock's fake, and as Sturrock lost way and headed back on his original tack, Mosbacher drove over him, killed his way further, and sailed into a secure lead. The race was over.

Intrepid rounded the first weather mark with a lead of fifty-three seconds, twenty-five seconds too much for *Dame Pattie* to reach with dirty air. On the reaching legs, Mosbacher sailed a direct course while Sturrock hunted for speed by reaching up. *Dame Pattie* rounded the bottom mark behind by 1:53. The air now dropped to about seven knots and *Dame Pattie,* lighter and with the same sail area as *Intrepid,* caught the phasings well. This time Sturrock drove her beautifully through the spectator wakes which were worse for her, again, than for *Intrepid,* and closed to 1:45. But Sturrock's mistaken wind-hunting in the previous downwind leg was expensive, and he went off on various courses again, losing a minute and thirty seconds. On the last leg, *Intrepid* gained thirteen seconds, and both boats had to weave their way through spectators to the finish line.

The press was more critical of the spectator fleet after the second race and generated the only interesting event in the third race. Moved to ardor by newspaper and radio criticism, the Coast Guard doubled its coverage and urged its fleet to more visible effort.

Sturrock tried the same start he had used successfully in the two previous races, but the wind was fairly fresh and his sails frustrated his

AMERICA'S CUP—1970
"Misty Start"
With a fogbank lurking on the horizon, Gretel II *beats* Intrepid II
*across the line by two seconds, well clear of any windshadow. Sailing
her own race to the weather mark,* Gretel II *rounded 1:54 in the
lead. But on the reaching legs, fog and* Intrepid *blanketed her,
and the race is cancelled.*

purpose; *Intrepid* quickly ate out a half-mile lead. As she beat up the final leg, an open-cockpit day sailer appeared on the course. The small boat was manned by three young men beginning the four-mile sail back to Newport. She was at least a mile ahead of *Intrepid,* and could easily have cleared her course by half a mile. Spurred by a righteous zeal born of the recent criticism in the press, a lieutenant commander in a helicopter spotted the small boat and set out to drive her off the course—which she was already leaving, downwind, at her maximum. As the whirlybird swooped over them, the thirty-knot downdraft from the blades capsized the hapless interlopers. Their beer, cameras, lunch, and radio sank while they retrieved the rudder, the floorboards, an oar, got the boat back on its bottom, pumped it half out and got the sail up again. Outraged at their temerity in trying to sail off the course, the pilot circled and returned to the fray. By this time, *Intrepid* was within a hundred yards, driving along hard on the wind toward certain victory, with her ten-ounce mainsail straining in a twenty-knot wind. Mosbacher and Romagna were alone in the cockpit, with the rest of the crew below manning their handles, unaware of the imminent drama.

As the indignant wasp fell on the small-boat offenders and capsized them again, the downdraft blasted *Intrepid,* driving her rail and deck under, blowing her mainsail out of shape against her runner backstay and bending her battens against it. As Romagna frantically paid out sheet and Mosbacher tried vainly to round up into the vertical gale, half a ton of water cascaded through her deck openings. The helicopter lifted as the pilot saw what he was doing, and *Intrepid* staggered back on her feet and swept on, her mainsail a little baggy, but slowly regaining its shape. *Intrepid* won by 4:51.

The final race was a walkover. Just before the start, both boats broke for the line on opposite tacks, and crossed well-separated at approximately the same time. As they came back and Mosbacher closed on Sturrock's tack, Sturrock again tried a fake tack and managed to make Mosbacher tack. But the fluky wind, wandering between five and twelve knots, died as he fell back on his original tack, and Mosbacher, over and filled away, swept out of Sturrock's control and never looked back. *Intrepid* was two hundred yards ahead at the first weather mark, three hundred at the bottom mark, a half-mile at the weather mark, slightly less at the final bottom mark, and finished, to the usual blare of whistles, firing of flares, cheers, and popping of corks, ahead by 3:35.

It must have been a dull summer for Mosbacher—lacking the excitement and tension of campaigning an inferior vehicle and winning by technique and tactics—sailing a series of routine triumphs. If anything can cure a sailor of America's Cup fever, it may be just this experience. At any rate, an easy winner, Bus handled his triumph with such grace, modesty, soft words, and kindly attitudes that he was thereafter made chief of protocol for the State Department.

Sturrock was also cured of the fever, and went back to Australia with a comprehensive and accurate recommendation. He made it quite clear to yachting magazines and the daily press that the Cup was not available to a merely superior boat and a good crew. The development, in real competition, of a highly varied attack, of a complete set of sails with well-known characteristics and trim, the training of specialists in trim, navigation, "calling," condition analysis, and optimum performance—all these might be a beginning. Perhaps more important, he suggested that several challenges might eventually bring together the understanding and attitudes that would, added to a summer's competition, assure success.

Baron Bich and Sir Frank Packer heard and understood, and the twenty-first running of the America's Cup would be a classic, a competition, and a threat to future defenders. Had it been run by two syndicates instead of two imperators, the challenge might have succeeded.

AMERICA'S CUP—1970
"America's Cup Buoy"
Gray skies loom over Gretel II *as she leads* Intrepid II *to the finish
line. An eight-knot breeze is perfect for her sails, and Hardy, behind
by a minute and a half after a collision at the start, has caught and
passed* Intrepid *with only the weather leg to go.* Gretel *won the
race, lost the protest.*

Chapter Five
A CONFUSION OF TECHNIQUES

The runaway success of *Intrepid* in 1967 shook designers everywhere, because she introduced several entirely new elements to twelve meter design. With the new trim-tab set four or five degrees to windward, *Intrepid* made two degrees less leeway, actually crawling up under the lee of another boat when she appeared to be pointing below her. Her knuckle bow increased her sailing lines, and the forty or so square feet that Olin Stephens cut off her keel area significantly decreased her skin friction. Since drag is relative to the square of the wetted surface times the square of the speed, that forty square feet made the winning difference. The third area of pronounced difference in *Intrepid* was her full afterbody.

The bow of a boat does two things to water: it splits it apart on either side of the hull and presses it down under the hull. As long as the change of pressure is gentle and constant between one section of a boat and another, the water continues to flow past the moving boat. Layers of water next to the hull flow more slowly than the layers outside them. This pattern is

AMERICA'S CUP—1970
"A Clear Win for Intrepid II*"*
An eighteen knot "smoky sou'wester" was Intrepid II's *wind, and
she crosses the finish line with just the hundred-yard lead she had
at the start. While the fifty-foot NYYC Committee Boat* Incredible
rolls and pitches, the Coast Guard's bark Eagle, *behind the line, sits
like a brick.*

called "laminar flow." As long as water passes the hull in laminar pattern, the resistance of the wetted surface is minimal. Where laminar flow ceases, small eddies start to form and roll down the hull at one-fourth to one-tenth the speed of the laminar flow, building up further eddies outside themselves. There is a physicist's rhyme which goes:

The littler whorls have greater whorls,
Which feed on their velocity,
And the greater whorls still greater whorls,
And so on, to viscosity.

The point where laminar flow usually ceases is the point where the hull begins to curve back toward the rudder. In late 1965 Pierre (Pete) DeSaix, of the Davidson tank, discovered that laminar flow stopped at the location of the quarter-wave on a Twelve's hull. He conducted a series of tests with bits of thread attached to the hulls, which made visible the direction and location of "separation," as he named the effect. Working from these visible indicators, Stephens moved the fullness of *Intrepid*'s hull further aft, thereby making the change of pressure gentler as the hull curved back toward the rudder. He also carried the fullness a little deeper, so that the water thrust down had a later and more oblique change of angle as it started up. Since everything done on a boat is a compromise, the gentler beginning of the taper aft meant a more abrupt turn at the stern. The stern of *Intrepid 1967* had a slightly pregnant appearance. By 1970, all the designers saw what Olin had done, and their own tank tests confirmed DeSaix's findings. As a result, sterns appeared which had the inflated appearance of a duck about to lay an egg. The irreverent press christened this feature "the bustle."

The key figure in the great bustle rush was the brilliant naval architect, Britton Chance, Jr., stormy petrel of designers. Tactless as he is talented, impatient as he is brilliant, and well-connected as a computer, Brit's career has bounced between disaster and triumph. Like Ted Hood and Olin Stephens, Chance is the son of a successful man who encouraged him; he has been a successful and skilled sailor since he could hold a tiller, racing before he was ten and skippering his family's yacht when he was eleven. When he was in his teens, he worked with DeSaix at the Davidson tank; and when he was twenty-one he took a job in Ray Hunt's office. When Hunt failed to pay enough attention to him, he left and went to work with Ted Hood's small design office where *Nefertiti* was conceived. Within a few months, he was back at the Davidson tank with models of *Nefertiti,* working round the clock with Hood in an effort to develop competitive twelve meter knowledge. In February, 1962, he left Hood's office to become a designer on his own.

Brit's first design was for his father, Olympic 5.5 meter champion in 1952. *Complex V,* built in 1963, placed third in the U.S. Nationals, and was second in the trials for selection of the defender of the Seawanhaka Cup. Brit's second 5.5, *Charade,* led the 1964 Olympic trials until the last race, when she was barely beaten by the other stormy petrel of yachting, Boston's Don MacNamara. By this time, Brit was working on twelve meter design on his own. He had won a $10,000 grant from the Twelve Meter Fund, established by the New York Yacht Club for twelve meter research, and was drawing lines and tank testing at Davidson.

Like the Twelves, 5.5 meter design is locked into the International Rule, and is a pretty good ground on which to test twelve meter design concepts. It is preferable to the towing tank, because it tests a model half the size of a Twelve in a liquid whose viscosity is comparatively realistic. At 0.9 inch to a foot, a tank model is sailing in a liquid which, relative to an actual Twelve, has the viscosity of crude oil. Brit's 5.5 designs won the world championships every year from 1967 through 1972, and in 1968, his 5.5 won the Olympics.

In 1968 and 1969, Brit was the key figure in twelve meter thinking. His 5.5s were significant models to which prospective twelve meter designers looked. Nothing Olin Stephens had de-

AMERICA'S CUP—1970
"The Race Gretel II *Won"*
Gretel II's *chance came late in the fifth race of the series, when*
fluky, dying air brought a trailing Gretel II *within striking range of*
Intrepid. *A ninety-degree windshift let* Gretel II *lay in the mark*
and win—and cost Intrepid *two tacks, a hundred yards, and*
the race. Here Intrepid *tacks into a lift as* Gretel II *pays off to*
cross to victory.

136

signed was as up-to-date or as publicly visible. And since the bustle was an increasing feature on Chance 5.5s, every twelve meter designer ran bustled Twelves through the towing tank, even Olin Stephens.

The success of *Intrepid* stimulated America's Cup ambitions to new intensity. Baron Bich, undeterred by what he had seen in Newport, applied his tremendous capacities to the task of creating a winner. Sir Frank Packer, with *Gretel* and the best challenging performance to date, sent Payne back to his drawing board and to the Aussie tank to prepare for the fray.

Baron Bich more or less set the pattern of action. He went to Brit Chance, under advice from the Le Guillou family, which had won championships with Chance 5.5s built by the Swiss boatbuilder, Herman Egger. Chance, of course, could not build the Baron a Twelve to compete for the America's Cup, since the designer and the builder had to be resident in France. But he could design a Twelve for Egger to build, and that Twelve, *Chancegger*, would provide a platform and prototype hull from which a French architect could extrapolate a possibly superior hull for the real contest. Meanwhile, to make sure that no opportunity was overlooked, Bich bought *Sovereign* and *Kurrewa V*, and now added *Constellation* and *Chancegger* to his fleet. He selected three full crews from a sizeable number of eager candidates and sent them to Hyeres to sail against each other, develop sails, learn techniques, and come up with suggestions. He also found three talented helmsmen to sail his craft. Louis Noverraz was a Swiss, the grand old man of European sailing, "the man of a thousand victories," and almost certainly Bich's best skipper. Poppy Delfour, the French 505 champion, had little experience in larger boats, but a strong sense of independence. Jean-Marie Le Guillou, like his father a 5.5 champion, was the third, and like Delfour, he had little experience in large boats; but unlike Delfour, Le Guillou was acutely aware of his own shortcomings and eager to learn.

The progress of the Baron's campaign greatly excited the curiosity of the rest of the world. One member of Packer's crew, in Europe for the world's 5.5 championships, managed to get a look at the hull of *Chancegger* while she was still under construction and carried the word to Australia. *Chancegger* was completed in time to race briefly against other boats in the Baron's stable. As an American designer, Chance had full access to Pete DeSaix and the Davidson tank during the development of the *Chancegger* tank model. The model was used extensively by French designer Andre Mauric in developing *France,* as the challenger was named. Mauric incorporated most of Chance's ideas about the breakthrough Twelve: as long a waterline as possible, weight-saving devices like a chine above the waterline, minimal rudder area, and pulling the maximum beam aft to lengthen laminar flow. *France* may even have been slightly more bustled than *Chancegger,* and she was fuller and flatter in the bow sections in order to increase her speed downwind and give her a fighting chance against a Stephens boat. As competition in Newport was to prove, *France* was faster than *Constellation* in over twelve knots of breeze. *Chancegger* was said to be a faster light-air boat.

One thing was clear to the Baron quite early, however; he invited Bob Bavier to race with his boats against his skippers in Hyeres. In three races, Bavier won once with each boat, demonstrating thus that there is no substitute for experience with a Twelve.

Meanwhile, Payne was quietly and thoroughly at work, and *Gretel II* was a very fast boat. Early reports from Australia were contradictory. She had no visible quarter-wave, so Payne seemed to have solved the "separation" problem. Further, she had no waterline—her hull and bottom were a uniform white, perhaps to prevent watchers from being able to see whether she was sailed to windward at a different fore and aft trim from her downwind attitude. She had a wheel on each side of the cockpit to enable the helmsman to see the genoa trim better, collapsible spreaders to allow closer trimming of the genoa, and a supermast, tapered and with little rivet-heads serving as vortex generators on its forward sides. About forty-five degrees either side of the centerline, they did something exotic to the airflow. A windtunnel test had suggested this stretching-

AMERICA'S CUP—1970
"Intrepid II *and* Gretel II"
Completing a tack in the second windward leg of the final race,
Ficker shoots Intrepid II *to the weather as his genoa fills. His runner*
tension will flatten his luffing mainsail. Hardy fills Gretel II *and*
drives off after his tacks.

for-effect. The Australian press, which was not unconnected with Sir Frank Packer, vociferously reported the information that *Gretel* frequently beat *Gretel II*. By the time Sir Frank announced his choice of crew and of Jim Hardy as helmsman, and sent only *Gretel II* to Newport, very few defense candidates believed much that had come out in the Australian press.

This major ferment did not go unnoticed in the United States, especially by *Intrepid*'s manager, Bill Strawbridge. Olin Stephens was already committed for a new Twelve to Bob McCullough, Vice-Commodore of the New York Yacht Club and a widely successful ocean-racing skipper. McCullough had signed on the most experienced Twelve crewmen in the country for *Valiant*, his new S & S boat. Even *Intrepid*'s skipper, Mosbacher, was not available to Strawbridge, as he was busy as chief of protocol.

Strawbridge made two moves to give his syndicate, which was virtually a rerun of the 1967 group, a fighting chance. First, he hired Brit Chance to bring *Intrepid* up to a competitive level with the new Twelves. Brit was aware that

Valiant and *Chancegger* had tested slightly faster than previous Twelves, but he also knew that *Intrepid* had a very good set of sails and a titanium rigging and upper mast section. Titanium was much stronger, ounce for ounce, than aluminum, and made *Intrepid* slightly stiffer than a new challenger might be.

Next, Strawbridge signed on San Francisco's Bill Ficker as skipper. Ficker, a former World's Star champion, a match-racing winner in the Congressional Cup Series, and one of *Columbia*'s helmsmen in Newport in 1967, was handed the task of developing an expert crew from scratch. With a couple of experienced hands like Steve Van Dyke as caller and Peter Wilson as navigator, he picked a group of young bachelors, fresh from college and experienced in ocean racing, and set about learning the rebuilt *Intrepid* and developing his crew.

As it turned out, Brit had made *Intrepid* faster than *Valiant* by modifying her in *Valiant*'s direction, but he stopped short of an extreme bustle. He lightened her rig by using her main halyard as the backstay, thus saving about forty pounds of

142

heeling moment. It says something for Brit's fantastic self-confidence that he did not attempt a breakthrough with the redesigned *Intrepid,* but was content with merely making her successfully competitive; after all, it was a Stephens design.

Ted Turner, World's Ocean Racing champion and owner of *American Eagle* (converted for ocean racing), was itching to get into real Twelves. He decided to form a syndicate of his own and build a Twelve which he would call *Shenandoah.* The syndicate never materialized however, since the seed money was to come from Turner and Perry Bass, Ted's navigator. At that point, Bass was more interested in building a maxi-ocean racer for Ted to skipper while he navigated. Even though the *Shenandoah* stake failed to materialize, Ted's infection was too great for him to stay out, and he brought *American Eagle* to Newport, and was laid on as a trial horse for *Gretel II.*

Meanwhile, the most unusual challenge of them all was building in Florida. Charley Morgan, sailmaker, designer, yachtbuilder, and ocean racer, set out to be a one-man contender.

Morgan is one of the country's great sailors and a master helmsman. He sailed in Tampa Bay, coming up through the small classes to become a sailmaker and skipper of ocean racers. From sailmaking, he went into designing and building ocean racers and finally into production-line sailboats. When he finally sold it in 1966, his Morgan Yacht Corporation was one of the largest in the country and certainly one of the most profitable. Morgan's dedication to sailing was so intense that his corporation published its own newsletter and his employees had their own yacht club and championship series.

Morgan had tried to put together a syndicate for 1967, but did not quite bring it off. By 1969, he had assembled a good crew and added to the initial group an enormously successful helmsman and ocean racer from Long Island Sound, Tom Young. Young invented and constructed a hydraulic lift so that *Heritage,* Morgan's contender, could be lifted out of the water between races and kept light.

Heritage was the most beautiful of the new crop. She was finished bright, and her varnished

AMERICA'S CUP—1970
"Rounding the Weather Mark"
Carried above the layline by Intrepid II, Gretel II *comes down on
the second weather mark with cracked sheets. Intrepid's genoa opens
as her foredeck crew readies her spinnaker.*

144

mahogany was matched and elegant. She may have been a fast boat, but the omens were against her. At her launching, the crane started to topple off the dock as she was being lowered overboard, and only the quick reaction of the operator, who dropped the boat before the crane overbalanced, saved *Heritage* from being sunk at her own launching. Then, her minor damages repaired, she was towed north, and had a rough time coming. When she finally arrived in Oyster Bay, she was three days late for the first races and not really ready for competition against *Intrepid, Valiant,* and *Weatherly. Heritage* served only to provide a new T.V. role for the America's Cup scene—the tragic hero.

Intrepid opened the Observation races with two quick wins over *Valiant* on June 8; *Valiant* came back on the ninth to beat *Intrepid* twice, winning the second race by only ten seconds. On the tenth, *Valiant* beat *Intrepid* by better than two minutes and finally, with Morgan sails against Hoods, the newly rigged *Heritage* entered the fray and lost in succession to both *Intrepid* and *Valiant. Heritage* ordered Hood sails and left

Long Island for Newport and extensive tuning. The final race of the June series was won by *Valiant,* and the openers for the 1970 season looked like a *Valiant* reply of *Intrepid*'s breakthrough years.

By the time the Long Island Sound races were over and the contenders moved on to Newport, observation, examination, and cross-reference had established that *Valiant* had a polymer bottom, titanium rigging, carbon-boron boom, and a spectacularly empty deck. So *Intrepid* got a polymer botton, as did *Heritage.* Meanwhile, *Weatherly,* still a good boat in very light air, was made one of the official contenders for the defense for a variety of reasons. The Selection Committee needed four contenders to pair off in the daily races. Moreover, noises were emanating from Australia, where Packer talked a lot about starting tactics and putting the aggressive Dutchman Martin Visser at the starting line on the crew of *Gretel II.* Probably the best starter in the United States was Commodore George Hinman, who had been involved as a sailor or a member of the Selection Committee for every

America's Cup in Twelves. With Hinman as *Weatherly*'s skipper and with a crew of slightly older sailors, most of them more accustomed to executive decision than pulley-hauley, the trials would go a long way to inure whichever contender was selected against any Australian fancy work at the starts.

By the first of July Newport was humming. *Heritage* still didn't satisfy Charley Morgan. Television crews, accurately estimating that Morgan would be eliminated in time for them to complete a show that could be televised during the week of the Cup Races, were filming his every move. Like many men of vast ability and inventiveness, Morgan had more ideas than he could handle and was moving in more directions than could be useful. His sails still needed full attention. He moved his mast forward, added thirty square feet to his total rig, took a twelve-hundred-pound slab of lead out of *Heritage*'s keel, and went on losing races.

Baron Bich did not fare much better. His three skippers were now down to two; Jean-Marie Le Guillou quit, having wisely concluded that the policy of keeping everyone in the air until the last minute might keep the crew on their toes, but wouldn't let a skipper get his boat decently tuned. The French were also enchanted by some enormous Herbulot spinnakers—possibly because they were decorated with enormous regional shields. American contenders had long since come to two conclusions about spinnakers—first, small ones worked better than big ones on Twelves, and, second, a plain white spinnaker told the opposition nothing, whereas a gaudy one identified itself and gave away policy.

Meanwhile, Chance remarked that *Intrepid* was really the fastest boat in Newport and would begin to show her stuff as soon as her green crew managed to sail her properly. *Weatherly* got a titanium-topped mast, *Valiant* broke her carbon-boron boom, and crews on all three American boats discovered that they could increase their downwind speed by bending their masts over their bows and setting their spinnakers farther forward. The titanium-topped masts would bend up to three feet out of line. Olin Stephens threw a little tremor into the opposi-

AMERICA'S CUP—1974
"Intrepid *and* Courageous—*Final Trials, 1974*"
In half a southwest gale, with the score tied, Hood on Courageous
uses a rejected Intrepid II *heavy mainsail to beat Driscoll and*
Intrepid/West. *Hood had skippered his own design,* Nefertiti, *in two*
attempts to defend, and had trimmed his sails on Vim. *Here, in*
command for the first time, he earns the defender's slot in one race.

tion by telling some reporters that "a three percent improvement in speed is the goal from one twelve meter to the next," and this ambitious announcement was solemnly printed.

On the fourth of July, three days before the Observation Trials, Harold S. Vanderbilt died. He was the reviver of the America's Cup Races, the king of the "J" boat era, the original author of the NAYRU yacht racing rules, and the inventor of contract bridge. Syndicate and national flags were flown at half-mast in all the Twelve camps.

The observation trials started on July 7, to drawn pairings. Racing in five to ten knots of fluky breeze, *Valiant* beat *Heritage* by 9:26, and *Intrepid* beat *Weatherly* by 3:55. On the ninth, *Constellation* beat *France* by 1:45. Poppy Delfour, at *France*'s helm, said she "steered badly"; Noverraz, driving *Connie*, said the air was fluky. In the American races, *Intrepid* beat *Heritage* and Charley Morgan said *Heritage*'s low-geared wheel was a mistake, that it had about as much feel as "doing pushups." *Valiant* beat *Weatherly* by two hundred yards in a fifteen-knot wind. *Weatherly*

took the start by quite a bit and *Valiant* didn't get her wind clear till halfway through the race. The tenth and the eleventh were fogged in, but on the thirteenth, *Intrepid* started under *Valiant* in light air, squeezed her up and beat her by two minutes. Then *Heritage* raced *Valiant*, made a good start, and in a race where the lead changed several times, *Heritage* won by 1:09. At this point the irreverent press suggested that Baron Bich and the managers of the *Valiant* and *Heritage* camps get better helmsmen. Actually, both boats had the same trouble—they were hard to settle into the groove after a tack, while *Intrepid* and *Constellation* picked up speed at once and steered easily.

The Observation Trials went on with no real change. From the fourteenth to the seventeenth, *Intrepid* won four, two from *Valiant* and two from *Heritage*. *Valiant* won one, and *Weatherly* won three, one on a protest against *Valiant*. On the last day of the Trials, the big switch came; *Valiant* and *Heritage*, both sailed evenly and well to windward, beat *Intrepid* and *Weatherly*, *Valiant* by 1:50 and *Heritage* by 3:41. The Selection

150

Committee had a lot to consider, and the following week's New York Yacht Club Cruise did not unlock their confusion. *Intrepid* won two races on bad tactics by *Valiant,* who set the wrong spinnaker too soon in one race and got shaved off in a start at the Committee Boat in another. These errors, plus five incidents involving fouls during the Observation Trials, could not have built confidence in *Valiant*'s tactical ability to defend the Cup.

The losers now began to panic. *Heritage* and *Valiant* went out to sail and came back to change the boats around. *Heritage* moved her rudder twelve inches aft and moved her mast forward. *Valiant* tried a bigger cavitation plate, filled out her aft waterline, and fattened her rudder with micro-balloons. *Weatherly* got a new mainsail, and Brit Chance, realizing that *Valiant*'s after fattening lengthened her waterline, fattened *Intrepid* by applying wide fairing strips that began on her fat hull and came well back on her thin rudder, thus extending the waterline between rudder and hull. Jeff Spranger, writing in the Newport *Daily News,* felt that the concentration had shifted from sailing to redesigning, and remarked:

> An America's Cup contender needs fastidious attention to details before she leaves the dock, and fastidious attention to the helm thereafter.

In contrast to the constant changes and confused policies of the French, of Morgan, and, to a lesser extent, of *Valiant,* Ficker and his *Intrepid* crew did one thing at a time. Work on *Intrepid* was scheduled and completed before 1000; at 1000, she left the dock and practiced as necessary until 1500, when she returned to the dock and organized the next day's duties. Her crew weren't "den-mothered" with strict training regulations, but were expected to keep reasonable training on their own. Every bit of equipment and every person who went on board was weighed every day, and the totals were totted and posted. Ficker, in real life an architect, was an expert at best-path programming.

Morgan's frenetic inspiration finally drove

151

AMERICA'S CUP—1974
"Maneuvering for Start in the Mist"
In the first start of the 1974 series, as golden light filters through the
southwest haze, Dennis Conner, starting helmsman on Courageous,
evades Hardy's cover by rounding America's Cup buoy one minute
before the start and sailing into the spectator fleet. Helmsmen can't
see around jibs, so bowman acts as lookout before start.

Tom Young off the boat. Bich's refusal to choose a helmsman and let him get on with suiting the boat to himself and training the crew defeated both his skippers before they ever started. *Valiant* simply wasn't a good enough boat, and her problems were compounded by too many simultaneous experiments toward a solution. The postmortem for *Valiant* was spoken by Gerry Driscoll, West Coast boatbuilder and tactician, who came aboard *Valiant* to improve her tactical decisions. As he prowled before the Observation Trials, he commented that there were "too many parts, too many sails."

Gretel II finally arrived on August 6. If the boats already in Newport had problems, *Gretel* had all theirs and more. She had to analyze and learn the Newport weather and water patterns, and she had to develop her sails for these particular patterns, which were quite different from Australian weather. The boat and the rig had to be tuned after the shipping and rerigging. Her crew had to sharpen their racing tactics, check the American and French boats to make sure no advantage was being taken of the rules, and find out about the skippers, the crews, and the sails and the boats she would face. In retrospect, one wonders whether we would have retained the Cup had Bich turned *France* over to Noverraz and Noverraz raced Hardy and *Gretel II* from June to September.

The final Selection Trials were anticlimactic. They began with the usual ritual in which *Intrepid* beat *Heritage* and *Weatherly*, and *Valiant* beat *Heritage* and *Weatherly*. The only surprise came in the *Intrepid–Heritage* race, when Morgan lost by less than one hundred yards in a race in which *Heritage*'s boat speed was as good as *Intrepid*'s. In the rest of the series, *Valiant* won the first match against *Intrepid* by forty-two seconds; *Intrepid* won the rest by a half-mile, by twenty-three seconds, by a half-mile, by 2:08, by forty seconds, and, finally, in a race in which *Valiant* took the start and contained *Intrepid* to the bottom mark, by 2:33. *Intrepid* proved she could win, that she could come from behind and win, and that she could manage tactical choices with sufficient exactitude. Newport blossomed with "Ficker is Quicker" stickers.

The series to select the challenger was rather sad. Baron Bich named Louis Noverraz to sail the first race, and pacified a petulant Poppy Delfour (who had "quit" and then been soft-talked back into the fold) by offering him the helm if Noverraz lost the first race. Noverraz spent two days tuning *France* and sailed one of the great light-air races of all time, only to lose by a fluke.

France was at her best in over twelve knots of air, and for the first selection race "the man of a thousand victories" had a maximum of five knots against *Gretel II*, who was at her best in light air. Noverraz was behind Hardy before the start. When Hardy broke for the line Noverraz fed off, gained speed, and, with *France* making a bit of wind for herself, crossed slightly behind Hardy and just after the gun in the windward position. Still holding high, Noverraz kept *France*'s speed up, while *Gretel II*, fed off to foot faster, created a bit of wind of her own and gained toward the mark, but fell below *France*. When *Gretel II* tacked, she couldn't cross *France*, but *France* tacked to cover her and survived a tacking duel as the air died almost completely. *France* rounded the weather mark about a minute ahead, but not more than four boatlengths. *Gretel II* passed *France* on the first reaching leg, and Noverraz managed to lay dirty air on the Aussies and beat them around the leeward mark. A vagrant wind picked *France* up to pace and she pulled out of reach on the windward leg, rounding 1:30 ahead. Here she set one of those vast, unfortunate spinnakers, trapping lots of air and killing the flow, and slowly the Aussies with their smaller sail came down on *France*. For a while it looked as though they'd get Noverraz, but he managed to get a little off to starboard of the mark and to jibe and sharpen a flow of air across his spinnaker acreage, reaching the mark with good speed.

As usual, the spectator fleet ran ahead of the competitors to get a good view of the final rounding. From the Coast Guard cutter behind both boats and off to the side, a fleet of about thirty boats was visible, rushing toward the mark and stopping with a great reversing of engines and belching of heavy diesel exhaust. A pall of

155

AMERICA'S CUP—1974
"Split Tack Start"
In the gentle haze that kept spectators from seeing much of the first
race, Conner's start put Courageous *one hundred yards to*
windward of Southern Cross, but left Hardy out of tactical reach on
the other tack. Twenty minutes later, driving off for speed,
Southern Cross *was ahead. In later races, Courageous got to*
leeward of the Cross early and squeezed her up.

exhaust draped the bottom mark, round as a gumdrop and about as permeable; into this, at the end of a tense afternoon of masterful helmsmanship, still thirteen seconds ahead, Noverraz sailed and died. The wind that a Twelve makes for herself by her forward motion faded for Noverraz. Hardy, a young and alert skipper, took the bottom mark wide and free, preserving his speed until he coasted clear of the glue, and carried his wind all the way home. That evening, Poppy Delfour retuned to the boat as designated helmsman for the second race. Said reporter Spranger: "The logic of the shift of helmsmen had the merit of a lead franc."

Another ghosting match was on in the second race. Hardy got the start and led by more than two hundred yards at the weather mark. Delfour managed to generate seven to eight knots of boat speed on the first reaching leg, passed the Aussies, whose sailhandling was ragged, and maintained his lead on the next reaching leg. But Delfour wasn't Noverraz to weather and couldn't put a cover on Hardy, who blew through him with better speed after each tack, and drew

ahead by slightly less than his first lead at the windward mark. Downwind, *France* set her spinnaker beautifully and gained about a hundred yards before the Aussies got going. *France* was close enough to lay a wind shadow that Hardy luffed up to avoid. Until the wind died, *France* still had the boat speed to get by, but when it came back, *Gretel II* filled first and went home from there. Delfour's reaching and downwind tactics had been as good as Noverraz's in covering and moving the boat to windward. It was a pity that Delfour would not share the helm and possible victory.

Noverraz sailed the third race; the winds blew up to about twenty knots, and *France*'s sails went out of shape at fifteen. *Gretel II* won a no-contest by 2:24, even though she finished the last three hundred yards with her tack fitting broken and her jib blowing up her headstay.

The final race was disgraceful. Because one of the members of the International Race Committee had to leave to keep an urgent appointment in Italy, the Committee started the race in light air and fading visibility. Baron Bich took the helm of *France*—more to prevent blame for loss of the selection races from falling on his helmsmen than in the belief that he could win when they could not. Before the race was well under way, visibility dropped to less than fifty yards. The spectator fleet, wholly unchaperoned in the gloom, closed in behind *Gretel II,* who was masterfully navigated by Bill Fesq as she sailed around the course out of sight of *France.*

There is no way *France*'s crew could have heard the bells at the marks over the exhaust noise of close to a hundred spectator craft motoring between her and the Australians. So, the Baron sensibly took evasive action and sailed home to Newport. No one in his right mind would want to sail a thirty-ton Twelve through dense fog and an unchaperoned and practically invisible flotilla of spectator boats. *Gretel II,* who had to be towed back, was barely visible at the end of her tow line, nor could the crew of the towing boat see the Brenton Tower until their bow was less than ten feet from it. Somehow, everyone managed to get in from a race that should never have been started, let alone continued. Yet, in spite of Bich's gallantry and his eminent common sense, he was gratuitously accused of abandoning the race; and Eric Tabarly, aboard for the first time as navigator, came in for a share of the criticism. The most expensive, best-planned, and most carefully mounted challenge had come to nothing.

Baron Bich's gallantry did not stop at taking responsibility for *France*'s loss. In the two weeks preceding the Cup races, he turned *France* and *Chancegger* with their crews over to the Australians to give them real competition in preparing to meet the Americans. *Chancegger*'s sails were American and kept shape in stronger winds, and she was also very fast in light air. *France* did four complete races, and *Chancegger* a great deal of tuning sailing. By the time the Cup Races came, *Gretel II* was almost as well prepared as she needed to be.

In addition to aiding the Australians, Bich had brought large quantities of French champagne to the U.S., and he threw an epic party in the Newport palace he'd chartered for his crew. There weren't enough champagne buckets in all

Newport for the supply, the food was magnificent, and the orchestras played till dawn. Jim Hardy's family make about a tenth of the wine in Australia, and the Aussies also gave a grand party—renting the Vanderbilt mansion, "The Breakers," for the occasion. The beef was flown from down under by QANTAS, the wines were excellent, and the speech made by Sir Frank Packer, if a little brutal, conveyed rough fellowship and sympathy for the French. The serious business of the racing would follow.

Chapter Six
CONTROVERSIES: *Gretel II*
Fights City Hall

The America's Cup is not only an occasion for an international gathering of yachtsmen, it is also an occasion for a gathering of the world's most (and least) competent reporters. Day after day, whether the weather is suitable for sailing or not, reporters must meet a deadline with "news." So heroes and villains are created from bare bones, social theories are justified, and pontifications are issued in impressive prose. Great yachting insights come from great reporters like Somerville, Aherne, Spranger, Cady, d'Alpuget, Mitchell, and Wallace. But "baseball reporters in sneakers" are quick to cast very rich men as villains or boobs (unless they own a chain of newspapers). Public services such as the Police, Navy, or Coast Guard, suitably engaged in maintaining order at the vast public gathering, are excoriated for "wasting the taxpayers' money." The New York Yacht Club Race Committee is attacked as a bastion of reactionary conservatives, dedicated to the preservation of their own undeserved advantages. Such printed opinions unfortunately have side-effects.

The 1970 preparations for the Cup Races had

AMERICA'S CUP—1974
"Spinnaker Set"
Just too far back to get Courageous' *wind,* Southern Cross *readies*
to round 1974's "big mama" windward mark as Courageous *sets a*
light chute and starts her genoa down. Courageous' *bowman hauls*
at her genoa; foredeck crew raises butt of pole.

162

AMERICA'S CUP—1974
"Spinnaker into Jib"
Rounding the last bottom mark in the second race, Southern Cross
releases her spinnaker from the pole and starts it down. Forty-five
seconds back of Courageous, she is starting a long tack to the west
and into the spectator wakes which chop up the sea in the foreground.

already seen a few of these side-effects. Baron Bich, who has done more for the economy of France than anyone since Renault, became for the French press the boob, villain, and, finally, welcher on his own challenge because neither the splendid old Swiss, Noverraz, nor Poppy Delfour could beat the Aussies. In the foggy *France–Gretel II* race, the U.S. Coast Guard wisely stayed out of decision making. To avoid being accused of "wasting the taxpayers' money," the Coast Guard covered these international eliminations so thinly that the spectators were left to their own obtrusive devices. Anticipating the torrent of criticism that had previously followed their efforts to control the first-day crowd, experienced officers managed to evade the Newport assignment, and sent a sacrificial, green ensign to the Newport ritual. All these factors combined allowed the press to generate further excitement, much of it eminently justified. Not very far behind the scenes, Sir Frank Packer expertly fanned the flames. A raucous old body, he never had a riper opportunity or a better time.

"Aggressive starting" was the rule of the day, and in the week before the Cup Races, Ted Turner gave Jim Hardy such vigorous drill that *American Eagle* whacked off *Gretel*'s backstay. At the final formal inspection of the competitors on September 3, the Australians protested mightily two of Brit Chance's devices: first, *Intrepid II* did not have an enclosed head, and second (and rather fundamental), filling out her afterbody until it was more than a foot wide at the rudder post, and then fairing it into a substantially narrower, tapered rudder with a three-foot-deep fairing strip constituted an extension of the waterline and should be so measured. Nor were the Aussies disposed to accept the approval of Chance's variations tendered by the New York Yacht Club's measurer. In the uproar that developed around Chance's abuse of the rules, the fact emerged that the Lloyd's inspector for "specifications for scantlings" in Australia was not in close communication with the Lloyd's inspector who passed on American machines, and the dark suspicion was voiced that there might be holes in the fence.

In the interests of justice and peace, the responsibility for the waterline decision was taken from the NYYC measurer and put in the hands of the IYRU, some of whose representatives also constituted the International Selection Committee. Chance, nobody's fool, gave the beleaguered Committee an "out" by going at the fairing with tinsnips and chopping it off so that it was below the waterline by an inch or so, and was thus within the legal definition of fairing and outside the legal definition of waterline.

Gretel II went through her inspection with no objections from the Americans. Just before the inspection, her mast was moved aft six inches, having been moved forward some thirty-four inches for the American waters. The whole business of mast position appears to be quite different for Twelves than for ocean-racing yachts of the same size—perhaps because ocean racers do not have to float 75 percent of their total weight in their lead keels and therefore can have finer hulls forward. At any rate, Morgan, Hood, and Chance, who had more experience in ocean racers than in Twelves, all veered toward the larger foretriangle, which has a bonus of increased, unmeasured sail area in the 30 percent overlap of the genoa, and found again and again that it slowed the boat. All the giant spinnaker experiments produced similar results. A Twelve hull is so finely balanced that only very small variations in proportions of hull or sail will contribute to Olin Stephens's objective of "a three percent increase in speed" between generations.

Nobody expected that *Gretel II* and Sir Frank Packer would win the argument about the waterline; but, with the fine-honed legal instinct of a businessman who had built an empire, Packer had put the New York Yacht Club in an awkward position before the races began. When they allowed the IYRU to pass on the legitimacy of *Intrepid*'s rudder fairing, the NYYC had, in effect, admitted that their traditional position of making the rules for their defense, then sitting as judge and jury while acting as advocates for their own side, smacked of arbitrary rather than evenhanded justice.

Gretel II's opening maneuver had the stamp of

AMERICA'S CUP—1974
"Courageous *and* Southern Cross *at the Finish*"
On a bright, hot day, Southern Cross *sails her best race, her second of the series, and finishes as* Courageous *drops her jib and shoots to weather. In light air,* Courageous' *bulge at the waterline entry pushes a heavy bow wave as she noses into leftover swells.*

GOLINKIN

a "Packerstan" directive. After a crowd of over a thousand spectator craft, a three-hundred-foot destroyer, and several large Coast Guard cutters spent about two hours chopping all over the course, the area was cleared, and the Race Committee assumed its station opposite the America's Cup buoy. The wind blew a steady cold, gray, twenty to twenty-five knots from east of south, and there was a good sea running, which added confusion to the lingering wakes of the spectators. From opposite ends of the line and fairly well back, Gretel II and Intrepid started toward the line, apparently to do a test run for a timed start. Ficker was on port, Hardy on starboard tack, beam-reaching toward each other at about ten knots. As they approached the line, Ficker, the burdened vessel, bore off to avoid collision. Hardy, aggressively attempting to get to closer quarters, bore off toward Flicker, who then altered course to windward just as Hardy did the same. Both yachts were now quite close. Ficker went up on the wind, still avoiding Hardy, who was also sharpening for the line on starboard tack. Ficker was now slightly ahead of

Hardy, and could not have evaded Gretel II by altering course again; so Hardy held on until things steadied down, threw his helm down at the last minute and passed under Ficker's stern. Gretel immediately broke out a protest flag, which had been in stops on the starboard (Committee Boat side) shroud. Intrepid followed with hers. Gretel's maneuver, which looked coincidental, was apparently deliberate.

When the New York Yacht Club Race Committee announced the next morning that both protests had been disallowed because "there was no indication either yacht had infringed any rule," Packer had made his point. The Club got an unsympathetic press, which was quick to point out that the NYYC were their own judiciary. Actually, the Race Committee were quite right—in prerace maneuvering, normal rules of the road prevail. The burdened vessel must stay clear, and the privileged vessel must hold course. A starboard vessel cannot, therefore, continually alter course to force a port vessel to tack. But the public response to this pair of protests made the next Australian maneuver almost impossible for the NYYC Race Committee to field with honor, and undoubtedly contributed to the establishment, for subsequent America's Cup contests, of a neutral International Committee.

The start of the first race went to Ficker. A good start is terribly important in a close race, but nothing can defeat perfect timing. The time-honored technique in a match race of getting on your opponent's quarter and riding with him can be defeated if he stalls out back of the line and then goes for it at the right moment. Since he will sheet home and accelerate earlier than the boat haunting his stern, he will already be ahead and can stay in the clear. If you luff up under him from astern and attempt to push him over the line, he may opt to go for it early, carry you across the line, and dip it and be away before you can see around his sails to determine whether you were over. If you come over and behind him from windward, he can run the line and cross at maximum speed with the gun, at least a boatlength ahead and in a safe leeward berth. Every attack has a defense, and the start is

won in match racing by the same tactics that win it in fleet racing—flawless timing, good boat speed, and the ability to do the unexpected.

Hardy managed to get on Ficker's stern with a bit over a minute to go; with thirty seconds to go and Ficker head to wind near the line, Hardy got way up, ran down the line with his sheets started, and went across with the gun. Ficker sheeted home at exactly the right time, got up to about eight knots on the way to the line, and went over slightly after the gun. He was forty yards to weather of Hardy, and going faster. Ficker knew from watching the French work against Hardy that *Gretel* could not point hard to weather and move well; so he took *Intrepid* and her superior sails as high as he could and made as much speed as *Gretel* while he pulled above her. *Gretel*'s genoa was not equal to the wind strength and blew too full, heeling her beyond her best sailing lines and causing her to buck heavily in the lumpy sea. *Intrepid* led at the weather mark by a minute.

Rounding behind *Intrepid,* and certain of her greater speed off the wind, *Gretel* broke out her

AMERICA'S CUP—1974
"Beat to Windward"
Sporting a Kevlar main for the final race in a strong breeze,
Southern Cross falls off to leeward of Courageous in the first
windward leg, and is thereafter unable to make competitive speed. It
is the only race of the series in which the Cross did not pass
Courageous on the initial beat.

172

spinnaker before she'd settled down to speed; it went up in confusion, slammed the pole against the headstay as the bottom of the bag popped full, and broke the pole. It was a virtual replay of *Weatherly*'s disaster against the earlier *Gretel*. It took Hardy's crew two and a half minutes to get the spinnaker down, the pole stowed and replaced, and the spinnaker reset—a remarkable performance under the circumstances.

Gretel gained on the rest of the leg, and was behind only by the time the broken pole had cost her when she rounded the wing mark. The wind was now up to a steady twenty-five with higher gusts, and the seas were bigger. *Gretel* was taking green water over her deck, mostly from the heavy wakes of spectator craft, who ignored Coast Guard directives and followed close behind *Intrepid*. The water now poured across *Gretel*'s deck and was washing the lubricant out of her winches. As she dipped through a swell her foredeck boss skidded on the oil and went overboard. Hardy jibed around and picked him up on the second try, but another two minutes were gone.

Meanwhile, a three-hundred-foot destroyer positioned itself directly to weather of *Gretel*, and the Woods Hole Coast Guard cutter, trying vainly to herd the spectators out of the way, sailed across *Gretel*'s bow. She fought gamely on, and set a smaller and flatter genoa at the leeward mark, but with the lubrication washed out, the pawls were hanging up so that she could use her winches only if they were managed very cautiously. Bouncing through the spectators' wash, she made it to the windward mark, rounded, and was now mercifully almost abandoned, as the spectator fleet rushed down to the bottom mark to watch from there.

Intrepid, her sea smoother, her wind clear, and the competition eliminated, made a safe and stately progress to the finish line and won by 5:52. *Gretel* suffered her final indignity when the press cutter steamed around her, across her bow, and up to the finish line in time to photograph *Intrepid*'s triumph.

Bill Strawbridge, *Intrepid*'s syndicate manager, took no joy in the victory. "The management of the race course . . ." he said, "was the worst ever. I don't think two boats can be expected to race a suitable race under such conditions."

The second race was more to *Gretel's* liking. The wind was down to a maximum of fifteen knots, variable from the south and southeast. The Coast Guard sent an experienced commander up from Washington; he doubled his coverage and issued directives which clearly stated where the spectators were permitted and where they would be liable-to-a-large-fine. Mercifully, the spectator menace was over for the series.

Sir Frank took Hardy off the starting helm and put on the impetuous Dutchman, Martin Visser. Visser didn't bother to be aggressive—he did a perfectly timed start and led Ficker across the line by two seconds, thereupon turning the helm over to Hardy. Hardy sailed his own race to the weather mark, concentrating on boat speed and setting sails that were exactly right for the wind. He stood Ficker off for about ten minutes in a tacking duel, and thereafter didn't have to worry. *Gretel II* rounded the weather mark ahead by 1:54—a safe margin in a steady wind.

But the Aussies hadn't learned their lessons.

They set one of those enormous spinnakers (borrowed from the French and probably illegal), trapped too much air, and were overtaken by *Intrepid* shortly after they rounded the wing mark only twenty seconds ahead. The air was dying and the fog rolled in, cutting visibility to less than fifty yards. The Americans blanketed *Gretel*, leaving her to wrestle with half an acre of damp nylon, and slid around the bottom mark with a forty-six second lead. The New York Yacht Club Race Committee (with no special appointments for the next day) cancelled the race right there, proving that Baron Bich had been more than justified in his criticism of the International Committee.

Both challenger and defender now had a lot to think about. *Gretel II* had great potential, and, in Newport as in Australia, she found it now and then and performed well above her average. But the Aussies still had not categorized their sails as to performance, and their sail choice depended almost as much on luck as on guidance.

The third race sailed (and the second one completed) was the pinnacle of confusion for the week. A sunny September twentieth dawned, and in the still air of early morning, *Intrepid*'s crew assembled at the dock. While waiting for the weigh-in, Steve Van Dyke, *Intrepid*'s tactician, was sipping from a can of Coca-Cola. For some reason, several thousand bees swarmed the waterfront that morning. One of them happened to light on Steve's Coca-Cola, and sat soaking up sugar and arrogance. As Steve raised the can to his lips, the bee stung him. It hurt, but Steve is a big boy and bravely contained his pain and took off with *Intrepid*. Instead of diminishing, the poison swelled up his entire face and neck, and he began to have a splitting headache just about the time *Intrepid* cast off her tow and was at the America's Cup buoy. A little palaver with the chase boat, *Melantho*, and people were really worried for him. He was picked off by a Navy helicopter and flown in to hospital. Toby Tobin, an America's Cup navigator from an earlier campaign and a *Valiant* veteran, came aboard *Intrepid* as navigator, and navigator Peter Wilson was elevated to tactician.

As the Race Committee dropped their anchor to establish the line and sent out the windward-mark boat, one of the spectator boats saw a large, round, rusty object bobbing up from the depths and backed away from it, nervously calling the Coast Guard and inquiring if it was a mine. The Coast Guard cutter herded the spectator fleet to a one-hundred-yard distance, the press boat closed with the Coast Guard and snapped pictures, but nobody really knew what it was. Fifteen minutes of impasse dragged by, and then syndicate member Thomas Clagett informed the Coast Guard that he had a mine expert aboard, was vectored into the target area, and lowered the expert over the bow in a bosun's chair. As the expert and the "mine" came nose to nose, it was announced that the object was a submarine net float from World War II. The Coast Guard towed it off, the Committee fired the ten-minute gun, and the most controversial start in America's Cup history was about to take place.

Once again, Martin Visser took the helm of *Gretel II* for the start, and this time he and Packer had devised the following master plan.

Visser would hang near the starting line, close to the Committee Boat, on starboard tack. From this position he would block Ficker by getting between him and the Committee Boat, or, if Ficker went astern of him, fall on Ficker's wind and get *Gretel* off with her wind clear and a slight lead. If *Intrepid* got on his tail, he would do a good timed start and either wipe *Intrepid* off on the Committee Boat or beat her across the line. The whole operation depended on Visser's timing, and the Dutchman was a master of precision starting. The one factor they failed to consider was a fishtailing breeze which blew from south and southwest at eight to ten knots, veering or backing as much as twenty degrees as it filled in; and it was this breeze that defeated Visser's plan.

Visser took his position with about a minute to go. Ficker, without his usual tactician, was doing a close-reaching timed start from behind the Committee Boat. *Intrepid* came toward the line at full speed with her sails free; as she came, Visser sheeted his sails in, hardened up, and tried to close the gap. At this point, the wind faded and swung twenty degrees from south to southwest; the stern of the Committee Boat swung toward Visser and *Intrepid*'s hole. *Gretel*, sheeted flat, slowed abruptly to five knots as she came into the lee of the swinging Committee Boat, and *Intrepid*, with her wind free and her sails hard full, accelerated toward the hole. She had all the speed she needed to shoot astern, around, and past the stalled Visser, but *Gretel* was so stalled by circumstances that the opportunity to go through her wind seemed too good to miss; so Wilson advised and Ficker went. Ficker was still a boatlength away when the gun sounded and the rules changed from the pregun situation to the race situation.

As Ficker entered the hole, he swung his bow up to get on the new wind, and as *Intrepid* blanketed *Gretel II*, the Aussie's genoa sucked up against her mast in the backwind of her forward motion. Visser never moved the helm, and *Gretel* banged into *Intrepid* aft of amidships, breaking off the tip of her bow. *Intrepid* swept across the line and as Hardy took *Gretel*'s helm, both protest flags were flying. Hardy sailed the race perfectly. First, he fed *Gretel* off for speed, and as Ficker freed his sheets a little and footed to cover *Gretel,* Hardy initiated a tacking duel, which Ficker broke off after twenty-four tacks. The start had cost *Gretel* about a minute and a half, and she rounded the windward mark forty-two seconds back. *Intrepid* made good speed on the two reaching legs, and *Gretel* gained about two boat-lengths, rounding, in freshening eight-knot air, about a minute behind. On the second windward leg, Hardy and Ficker simply sailed for speed, and Hardy pulled up to within two hundred feet of *Intrepid,* who was now only thirty seconds away and within reach of *Gretel's* wind shadow. Downwind, both boats reached away from the mark in quest of speed and weather gauge, but it did Ficker no good. As they jibed back and forth, *Intrepid* to escape and *Gretel* to lay the pauseful finger, *Gretel,* now steered by Olympian downwind expert David Forbes, closed the gap. With half a mile to go, she passed *Intrepid,* rounded one hundred yards in the lead, and never looked back, winning by 1:07.

The spectators were overjoyed as *Gretel* came across the line, and the excitement included several flares, at least a hundred cans of instant noise, and cheers that hit about seven on the Richter scale. But the joy hardly lasted to the dock. The protest, couched in grimmest prose, awaited the end of the day.

A competitor who brings in a protest plays the following game: he tries to have the protest judged according to a rule favorable to him, and to avoid the rule favorable to his opponent. The Committee tries to find hard evidence and to match the situation to the appropriate rule. Like most protests, each side had its own version of what actually happened. Ficker, an architect by profession, made a neat, properly statistical set of presentation drawings which were accompanied by a written text that was legally airtight. The Australian sketches bore only a distant relationship to the incident-according-to-Ficker. On the morning following the race, Chairman B. Deveraux Barker opened the meeting with friendly informality. Within minutes, Bill Ficker took over the meeting with the ease and grace of a man accustomed to running things. Visser protested the casual air, forcing Barker to resume control and conduct the meeting in strictest formality.

The evidence of the contestants was contradictory. The Race Committee had had an eyeball-to-eyeball view of the collision, but to reach a decision an answer had to be found to the following question: was *Gretel II* pointing above a fair course to the next mark at the moment she struck *Intrepid?* In order to answer that question, the Committee would have had to be up close and four miles away simultaneously or aboard *Gretel II* and looking at the next mark; therefore, no one on the Committee could be a reliable witness.

The question was finally decided on the strength of a series of aerial photographs taken by Newport photographer John Hopf, a long-time yachting fan who regularly covers the America's Cup Races from his photo-plane. Hopf was above and slightly behind the Committee Boat

Incredible as *Intrepid* started through the gap. He took a series of seven photographs as the incident developed. The pictures showed *Gretel II*'s jib aback before she hit (or was hit by) *Intrepid.* With Hopf's pictures, the Committee felt they had no choice but to find in favor of *Intrepid.*

Although *Gretel II* crossed the finish line first, Packer managed to lose the race, first by legislating the sailing on the course before the start and then by engineering a protest. Even in the process of losing, however, Packer once again exposed the New York Yacht Club's Achilles' heel, and no matter what decision they reached, they appeared as judges in defense of their own cause—home-town umpires.

The press and the public were far from receptive to the decision—not so much because it was wrong as because the Club had handed it down in their own favor. The public's failure to pay attention to the rules and to be out of sympathy with the rulers was illustrated in a letter to the Committee from someone who said, according to Geoffrey Hammond, historian of the America's

Cup, "The whole mess would not have happened if the Committee boat had not been in the way."

Rule 42.1 of the IYRU is as follows:

When approaching the starting line a leeward yacht shall be under no obligation to give any windward yacht room to pass to leeward of a starting mark surrounded by navigable water. But after the starting signal a leeward yacht shall not deprive a windward yacht of room at such a mark by sailing either above the first mark, or above close hauled.

The Committee decided that Visser was above close hauled after the smoke of the gun was visible and before he hit *Intrepid*. The Australians did not accept this verdict as being wholly candid. They claimed they were on a "fair course," that the shifting wind and the swinging Committee Boat made it impossible to ascertain the facts fairly, and that their maneuver, which they had attempted within the prescribed conditions of Rule 42.1, left unanswered questions about *Intrepid*'s behavior. For instance, if the wind shift put *Gretel II* head to wind, didn't it also put *Intrepid* in a bearing off position? Wasn't *Intrepid*'s genoa blanketed by her mainsail at the time *Gretel*'s genoa was knocked through her foretriangle? And didn't the prevailing wind pattern on the water show that *Gretel II* was not head to the wind that created those waves? Ironically, these questions were identical with John Hopf's opinion from his own pictures, and from his vantage point. And so it stands. No one will ever sort out the truth of the matter, but everyone in Newport was certain that the Australians were better advised to win the America's Cup by outsailing *Intrepid* than by trying to beat the NYYC Race Committee.

The third race went off without incident. The bees had returned to base, wherever it was. Hardy had the helm at the start. It was a warm, hazy day, with a true smoky sou'wester blowing between fifteen and twenty knots. Hardy got on Ficker's stern with about two minutes to go. Ficker did a tack and a jibe in an "S" pattern with his trim-tab cranked in and was free and headed away from the line. Hardy didn't want to get dragged too far away from the gun, and broke for the line early, whereupon Ficker came around onto the wind from his jibe, sheeted home, and drove after Hardy, falling off below him as though to run the line waiting for the gun. But when he closed below Hardy, he headed *Intrepid* up to stall Hardy at the line. Hardy crossed early, Ficker with him, but Ficker dipped back over the line, jibed, and crossed again first, a hundred yards to windward of Hardy and slightly ahead. Hardy put *Gretel* through a twenty-tack duel, but to no avail; Ficker broke off and simply sailed for speed, rounding the weather mark with a forty-eight second lead. *Gretel II* reached well, and rounded the bottom mark after two reaching legs without gaining or losing, still forty-eight seconds behind. The second weather leg showed no change, and, at the weather mark, *Gretel* was still forty-eight seconds back. Hardy now went for desperation tactics—there is little choice in a steady wind when the other fellow is just out of reach. He reached back and forth on the square leg, while Ficker ignored him and ran straight downwind for the bottom. Ficker was right; his margin had increased to 1:16. He gained two more seconds on the final leg to windward. The race had proved that the two boats were now exactly matched for speed in a fifteen- to twenty-knot wind. A little less wind, and *Gretel* was very dangerous. A lot less and she was more so.

With the score at three to zip, Ficker and Hardy came to the line on September 24 with Ficker plainly ready to write the Aussies off. He refused to tangle with Hardy at the start, and the two boats crossed the line close to the gun, *Gretel II* on port tack and *Intrepid* on starboard, about five seconds apart. The Newport wind was phasing about fifteen degrees, and Ficker sailed his windward legs independent of Hardy, tacking in headers and sailing into lifts. Ficker led around the course and Hardy followed, with the margin increasing from something like fifty seconds at the first windward mark to 1:02 at the final bottom mark. The loose cover Ficker had on Hardy proved Ficker's undoing in the final leg. He was the victim of a ninety-degree windshift.

In the final windward leg, as the breeze faded from about twelve knots to six or less, *Gretel* closed to within a hundred yards of *Intrepid*—a long distance under such light conditions. To visualize what happened, put your two hands about a foot apart and point them both to the left. Your left hand is Ficker, leading; your right is Hardy, perhaps two minutes back. Now rotate your hands through ninety degrees until both are facing ahead. Your hands are now equal—but the situation on the course was not. At the time the round-up happened, the competitors were on the tack parallel to the finish line rather than the tack toward it, and the round-up put Hardy almost laying the mark. He squeezed everything he had out of *Gretel II*, and she ate her way along even-steven toward the finish line. Ficker, making a desperate gamble, tacked in the hope that as he came parallel with the finish line, the wind would shift back. But for the first time his estimate of the phase pattern was incorrect, and a hundred yards from the finish Ficker on starboard tack couldn't squeeze the few feet he needed to force Hardy to tack. He had to dip under Hardy's stern as the area beyond the finish line, packed with spectator craft, exploded in anticipation of a victory that no Committee

could take away from the Aussies. It was the most spontaneous and frantic demonstration ever seen at a Cup Race. The Aussies were exultant as they crossed the line a minute later to win by 1:02.

The final race of the 1970 series was one of the most brilliant ever sailed. Again and again, less than a boatlength separated Hardy and Ficker, and through it all the Californian and his tactician, Van Dyke, earned their victory by their skill and judgment against a persistent opponent.

Hardy won the start. The wind was fluky, substantially north. *Gretel II*, making a timed start, forced *Intrepid* to the line, sailed across her stern, and shot through a length to windward and slightly ahead. Both boats sailed independently, as they had in the previous race, but this time in the lighter wind *Gretel II* eased ahead by about two hundred yards. Ficker found that boat speed was not the answer and set about distracting the Australians, using the irregularities of the wind. Ficker tacked, and Hardy tacked to cover. As the two boats tacked slightly out of phase with one another, the wind shifts were predominantly lifts for Ficker and headers for Hardy. Three hundred yards from the weather mark, as Hardy was headed yet again, he tacked in the hope that he'd get a port tack lift while *Intrepid* got a starboard tack header. But the wind held steady, and as the boats closed toward each other, it was plain that *Gretel II* could not cross *Intrepid*'s bow; her best hope would be to tack under *Intrepid* in a safe leeward berth.

Having closed, Hardy took his tack in a long looping turn. From astern and to windward, *Intrepid* drove off. *Gretel* needed to get up to speed, but before she could accelerate, *Intrepid* was abeam and in command. A short hitch to fetch the mark and clear her wind cost *Gretel II* a fatal hundred and fifty yards, and *Intrepid* held this lead down the two reaching legs to the leeward mark.

On the second windward leg, Hardy almost caught Ficker. Each boat sailed the leg independently, tacking on headers and playing the breeze for boat speed. Ficker became increasingly aware that he couldn't cover a boat four hundred yards away, and as the leg developed, *Intrepid* went west on a lift, and *Gretel* went east on a lift. If Hardy's lift died and he had to tack, he would be half a mile behind. If Ficker tacked to cover Hardy, he might have barely enough lead left to edge Hardy out at the mark. Ficker lost courage first and tacked, headed almost at the stern of the still-lifted Hardy. Earlier *Intrepid* had been lifted into the lead. As Hardy's lift faded, Ficker's lead was too much for *Gretel* to overcome. When *Intrepid* crossed *Gretel*'s bow, the Australians had made up all they had lost since the beginning but they were still short by one hundred yards.

The last mile of the weather leg was a furious tacking duel, and as the wind held steady and light, *Gretel* gained. In six tacks, *Intrepid*'s lead was down to a boatlength and *Gretel* tried to drive through. *Gretel*'s final chance depended on forty feet of water. For ten minutes Hardy tried to will his boat up under and ahead of *Intrepid*, to dump the backwind on Ficker that would keep *Gretel*'s hope alive. But Ficker was slicker and used Hardy's own concentration to defeat him.

Ficker carried *Gretel* beyond the layline, which gave him a hundred yards on her when he finally went for the mark.

That hundred yards was enough to get *Intrepid* home safe. On the square leg, *Gretel* carried *Intrepid* out east and closed to within thirty yards, but not quite close enough to lay a reaching shadow on her. Thirty seconds of blanket would have given *Gretel* a lead at the mark, but it was not to be. *Intrepid* rounded safely ahead, and a thirty-degree windshift made the final leg into a close reach, where *Intrepid*'s speed exactly matched *Gretel*'s. *Intrepid* finished with her lead intact, and the series ended by a 1:44 margin.

For the second time, Payne had produced a superior boat, and for the second time the summer-long testing and developing of the American crews and sails had kept the Cup. The Australians did not have long enough in American waters to learn their boat, their sails, or the local weather. Hardy's rapid progress gave every indication that he could have been a dangerous competitor with a little more ripening in combat and a little less interference with his priorities.

Conversely, Brit Chance's improvements on *Intrepid* were the margin by which the U.S. retained the Cup, since *Valiant*'s losing times to *Intrepid* were greater than *Gretel II*'s. The races against *Valiant* were the means by which Ficker's "green crew" achieved competence and confidence.

The 1970 series produced at least one victory for future challengers. Thanks to Packer's strategy, the protest committee would be a neutral international group, and the conditions for the challenger and the defender would be cross-checked by a single, neutral authority.

Chapter Seven
THE WINNING FORMULA—
THE LOSING FORMULA:
Preparing for the 1974 Challenges

The unspeakable arrogance of a century and a quarter of unbroken wins constitutes a challenge to the world; the procedures behind the successful American defenses are candid and undisguised. Yet the preparations for the 1974 races represented a cross section of approaches to the problem—good, bad, and noncompetitive. After five campaigns in twelve meters, the state of the art of design and campaigning had undergone definitive development, and any close observer of the Newport scene should have been able to compare campaigns and to derive the winning and eschew the losing formula. Yet the *Mariner–Valiant* group did a Charley Morgan and were still redesigning when the guillotine fell. Alan Bond, builder of cities and financial empires, personally conducted the most extravagant campaign in the long history of the America's Cup and put too much money in the wrong places. Baron Bich deliberately put his challenge on standby, and merely exposed a naive crew to a preview of future problems. Sparkman & Stephens, as usual, ran the *Intrepid* and *Courageous* syndicates through intelligently budgeted

185

shows which brought both boats to peak form and defended handily.

If the history of twelve meter campaigns had shown nothing else, it should have made clear to percentage players that Sparkman & Stephens, even if they do not win every time, always have one design in the final races for the defense selection, and often, both. Any wise campaigner who plans to defend or lift the Cup should choose an experienced designer to make him a new or a redesigned Twelve—preferably a designer with a leash on a superhelmsman.

The deserved popularity of the S & S office gives them certain built-in advantages. They know that one or two twelve meter contracts will be in the hopper before the current campaign ends, so they have a subdesigner checking out new ideas and experimenting with interim designs while the current ones are building. Then, for each contract, there is a project supervisor who runs a single campaign from the signing of the contract through the tank, the lofting, the building, the celebrating and the gift to a tax-deductible institution. This technique keeps the

twelve meter data in as few heads as possible, so there are few chances of security leaks even between rival contenders in the S & S office.

Once someone with sufficient resources decides to put together a syndicate, he needs a well-known designer and a proven skipper so contributors will have some inkling of the concentrated and dedicated teamwork that will consume their funds. It's not a bad idea to have the nucleus of a crew already committed, too: a good tactician, a sailmaker, a navigator, a foredeck boss, a starter, a spinnaker man, grinders, tailers, a sewerman, and a coach. Most potential contributors to a syndicate own ocean racers, and know that experienced crews are committed well in advance of any major race or campaign. They value experience and practiced teamwork.

The choices currently available for designer, project manager, skipper, and crew necessary to campaign a Twelve are extraordinarily limited. The twelve meter club is an exclusive organization; only three living men have designed successful Twelves. If Olin Stephens, Brit Chance, and Alan Payne are signed up, the syndicate manager must find someone with strong, recent success in ocean racers and take a shot in the dark. To make his chances a little less dark, he reflects that a superior skipper and an experienced crew can make a weaker boat strong enough to win, and he looks for any helmsman with a worldwide reputation and recent experience—a star of first magnitude rather than a comet blazing in the current sky.

The boat is built, a select group of five or six hundred celebrates her launching, and the initial experimental races are sailed in Long Island Sound; then boat, crew, and supporting staff go to Newport. The syndicate must now rent apartments for the married crew who cannot afford their own and take over a mansion for the rest (or a mansion big enough for everybody). They will need cooks, maids, a laundress, and a secretary. Local automobile dealers are happy to provide a pickup with the syndicate logo on the doors and the syndicate color on the body, but the crew and the shore groups will need pants, chemises Lacostes, sweaters, float coats, rain gear, and blazers with the appropriate color and logo. A tender, a chase boat, a shed, docking space for the fleet, and a sailloft will complete the ground–sea support. A reasonable supply of CB radios with one or more private crystals will ensure the secrecy of communications between the coaching boat and the Twelve. The shed will house whatever tools are necessary, as well as replacements for all winches, sheets, guys, shrouds, masts, booms, blocks, and instruments which will deteriorate with time and use. The sailmaker and the designer must have computer access as their statistics develop. About two years lead time is required for an on-board computer programmed for complex functions, and the team must practice judging the reliability of its answers. Together, the challengers and the defenders will share the costs of a P.R. man, his office, his telephones, his staff, and his duplicating machines.

The State of Rhode Island will make the Newport Armory available, and the various press agencies will fill it with teletypes, darkroom facilities, phototransmitters, a refrigerator for beer, typewriters, a coffee machine, soft-drink dispensers, and security guards. Press passes will be issued separately by each syndicate and by the press secretary, and a press boat will be laid on, for which the newspapers will pay the tab. The Coast Guard's Block Island boat will join the local boat, and a couple of eighty-footers will be moved to Newport for the preliminaries. By mid-June, Newport's 250 marina slips will be filled for the duration, the harbormaster will have assigned every available mooring; strange ferroconcrete ketches from New Zealand, Capetown, and Tahiti will anchor off and disgorge cinnamon-brown, bearded "writers" in tattered denims. Discotheques, boutiques, popcorn stands, leather shops, and silk-screen emporia will rent store space and lay hopeful traps for tourists. Bartenders, waitresses, and rock groups will migrate to this temporary mecca, and a Cup Summer begins.

In this milieu the syndicate and the challenger pursue their search for the elusive tenth of a knot which constitutes the difference between every other present-generation contender and the winner of this campaign. The key man is the skipper, who must be backed up by enough experts to convert his highly developed sensitivities into statistics and patterns. For this task, two sailmakers are worse than one sailmaker; two tacticians have a built-in fatal delay; two helmsmen can't tune a boat. A single, experienced, dedicated, and well-organized skipper is the touchstone for success.

In the sailing world, as in every other, the physical qualities of things constantly change. Consider sailcloth, for example. In 1964, a Hood mainsail for a Twelve weighed 12 ounces per yard; in 1967 it weighed 10; and in 1970, 7.6. In six years, cloth technology saved sixty pounds aloft and thus on an average lever arm of a third the mast height, saved some eighteen hundred pounds of heeling moment. Working from Hood specifications, duPont improved the basic form of Dacron polyester and reduced the stretch by 25 percent. In preparation for the 1970 defense, duPont did thousands of dollars worth of research and developed twenty-nine different varieties of Dacron fiber to meet the specifications of different sailmakers. For each Twelve, a sailmaker

buys a couple of thousand dollars' worth of du-Pont fiber, weaves or has it woven into cloth according to his own rigid specifications, and creates a sail inventory worth about forty thousand dollars. Then skipper, sailmaker, and coach sail every day and reshape by night, going down the long road of sail development until they know exactly how each sail will perform and under what conditions it will keep its shape and do the job.

"Too many sails, too many problems" may have been *Constellation*'s drawback through most of her trials. It was also Gerry Driscoll's opinion of *Valiant*'s weakness. During the 1962 series, *Gretel I* had eighty-five sails in her locker. Hood estimates that around twenty sails are all that can be developed effectively in a season. A competitive locker includes two or three mainsails, six spinnakers in various shapes and weights, eight genoas, a reacher, a drifter, and a few staysails. So far, no one has successfully used a blooper, probably for the same reason that giant spinnakers don't work with the Twelve's three-quarter foretriangle.

Sails work in conjunction with a hull, and each hull has its own pronounced characteristics. For example, in the 1975 World's One-Ton Championships at Newport, George Tooby did very badly in the first two around-the-buoy races with *America Jane III*. In the third race, he came around the bottom mark in about fourteenth place out of eighteen boats, and had no room to get immediately on the wind, as there were five other boats just ahead of him. He took *America Jane* wide to get into clear air, found that when he footed for speed instead of pointing high he went much faster, and he finished third. The next two races he finished second to Lowell North, the winner. *America Jane II* had been an exceptionally weatherly boat; *America Jane III* was a faster boat, but even with her sails full and looking functional, she died competitively when she was asked to go three or four degrees higher than she liked. Her sails, of course, were cut to Tooby's taste, and Tooby's taste was formed by his previous boat. So would *America Jane III* be ever faster if her sails were cut a little fuller? Such questions must be asked, answered, and accounted for in sail and tactical changes before any boat reaches her potential.

Each change in a sail results in a slightly different feel in the helm, and in a different balance of the forces generated by the hull. As the summer progresses, the helmsman has the subtlest computer of all, the human mind, programmed to analyze what is happening to his Twelve.

During the initial process of working up a boat, the crew takes her out and sails under close observation. A coach follows the Twelve through her various maneuvers, talking with an adviser in the observer's cockpit behind the helmsman. From the chase boat the coach, a role frequently played by the designer, takes readings of the wind strength, sticks a protractor against the windscreen of the chase boat to determine the degree of heel, and suggests changes in sail trim, leads, mast bending, boom bending, hoist tension, and Cunningham tension. The boat is tacked and the same tensions are tried on the other tack. Notes are made, and the helmsman reports how the boat feels, while the computer reports how close the boat is to her programmed potential.

Back at the dock, the designer and the helmsman consult with the sailmaker and the project supervisor. The mast may be shifted slightly, ballast taken out or added, the draft moved forward or aft in some of the sails, or the crew weight shifted for different points of sailing.

Gradually, as performance is evaluated, the emphasis shifts from the sails and the boat to crew performance. *Intrepid 1974* laid out a triangular course about a half-mile to a side, and spent at least one morning a week belting around it while her coaches watched from the chase boat and made suggestions about handling techniques, take-down procedures, and the positioning of crew. To go repeatedly from beating to reaching to running to beating in a mile and a half will standardize the performance of the crew and put them in combat condition.

As crew performance is honed to a fine edge, and sails begin to look as though they cannot be improved, the first trials come up, and gold is separated from dross. In recent years, the most

successful skippers are those who concentrate primarily on boat speed and take tactical and navigational advice in their stride. If the boat fails to reach her design potential, the skipper may be replaced by one who can generate more boat speed.

By 1974, American skill, technology, and management had been refined and reduced to a winning formula. Probably the biggest mistake the losers made was to require helmsmen to compete, even alternate, for the skipper's slot. Baron Bich is the classic example—and his boats never found their groove. The competition between Noverraz and Poppy Delfour prevented each man from fully utilizing his own skill in his own boat with his own crew. The brief nature of the challenge inhibits the full development of the challenging crew. They have a shorter experimental period than the native crop, and they lack the advantage of repeated racing for selection. As a result, both crew and skipper concentrate less, attain less psychic force, and sail in an atmosphere just short of high tension.

Even so, something about the international

stir of an America's Cup series stimulates imaginations and ambitions all over the world, inevitably luring a spate of challenges from likely and unlikely places. Geoffrey Hammond, in *Showdown in Newport,* sees this challenge as a product of social ambition. I have a faint feeling that few people in the rest of the world regard public attention in the United States as shedding social luster on anyone. But as a series goes on, and the dimensions and techniques of the challenge appear in oversimplified form in the press, people who have been successful in complex fields feel the double attraction of being challenged by the historical improbability of winning the Cup and the apparent simplicity of the mistakes made by the challenger. Instead of the tangled confusion of running a chain in tea and groceries, building cities, mines, or amassing a media empire, here is a fine, tight, complex, beautifully limited problem, with the modified scale, intricacy, and functional appeal of a ten-bladed jacknife to a boy scout.

Immediately after the 1970 races, challenges for 1973 were received from Canada, Italy, England, France and both sides of Australia. At a projected expenditure of approximately one million dollars per candidate, it looked like a six-million-dollar attack. The New York Yacht Club would have two new candidates—say two million dollars' worth—and *Intrepid* had been redesigned and was being rebuilt. Financially, the challengers were storming the bastions at the rate of better than two to one. Planning a challenge, however, is easier than actually raising the money and acquiring the necessary personnel. The Italians and the Canadians faded first. Then the British, whose Royal Thames challenge had been officially accepted on condition that they would run the elimination trials, asked for a postponement until 1974. The New York Yacht Club eagerly granted their request. The defeat of the new S & S *Valiant* by the 'Chancey' *Intrepid* had inhibited fund raising for a new S & S Twelve. This, coupled with a stock market decline, considerably dampened enthusiasm for a 1973 challenge.

After the postponement, Sir Frank Packer announced that he would not challenge again, and he did not live until the next races. In 1972, Baron Bich announced that the world's best known supersailor, Paul Elvstrom—"the Great Dane," builder, sailmaker, champion sailor, and winner of four Olympic gold medals—would be his skipper for the next Cup races and would also serve as "project manager" (a euphemism for running the whole show in company with some sort of tame French designer and boatyard).

If the publicity Bich drew for escaping from the fog was bad, the swarm of bees released by this announcement was catastrophic. Young French sailors and ambitious helmsmen who had hoped to take the wheel of the next French challenger were outraged; the press was horrified; the French government threatened to investigate the venture's tax status. But the trouble in France was nothing compared with the trouble Elvstrom himself gave Bich.

First, Elvstrom took *France, Chancegger* and *Constellation* to Denmark. He rebuilt *Constellation* so she would rate as a thirteen meter and be a faster yardstick for a new Twelve. He moved all her winches below deck and converted her

wheel to a tiller and a hiking stick. All the next spring she sailed with the crew below decks and Elvstrom sitting outboard on the rail, looking "as though he'd been shrunk for a horror movie." Then he sent *Chancegger* and *France* back to France under tow through the North Sea in the dead of winter. *France's* forty-thousand dollar mast went overboard and *France* sank. *Chancegger* fled into port and eventually got back home. *France* was recovered a month later at considerable expense. Meanwhile Elvstrom built a fancy spar for *Constellation* at one of his own subsidiaries in France at three times the cost of a usual twelve meter spar, and then managed to break it and lose it overboard in September. Bich had plans for a new aluminum Twelve to be built in Egger's French yard, when word leaked out that Elvstrom was tank testing a Twelve design of his own in a Danish tank. With the Cup races less than a year away, in October 1973 Bich cancelled building and informed Elvstrom that he was out of the operation.

France was restored after her sinking and slightly modified by her designer Mauric, and would be campaigned in 1974. Her skipper would be Jean-Marie Le Guillou, who had walked away from the 1970 challenge when Bich refused to end the game of rotating skippers. Le Guillou was a skilled 5.5 meter sailor; his family had steered Bich to Brit Chance; and Jean-Marie had deliberately disqualified Elvstrom in the 1972 Olympic Soling races by sailing the series as a grudge match, finally forcing Elvstrom to hit a mark. Designer Mauric's star was in the ascendant as well. His *Impensible* won the Half-Ton World's in August 1973; the defending champion, Elvstrom's *Bes*, failed to place.

Meanwhile, Australian attentions were focused on Alan Bond. He was the first Australian to get a tax write-off for a Cup venture, and he used it to publicize his Yanchep Sun City, an attractive development built on some sand flats about forty miles from Perth. He purchased *Gretel II*, and in his first public statement he proclaimed that his crew were going to be "all winners."

Bond had impressive qualifications beyond financial success and a considerable fortune. Be-fore the 1974 races, he had built, campaigned successfully, and participated in the design consultations of three ocean racers. His *Apollo II* was the size of a Twelve and had given him some sense of a Twelve's problems. He knew a number of practiced and capable ocean racers in Australia and could round up a competent crew. He was a tough competitor, a noisy, generous, outgoing man, and it was fun to sail with him. On the other hand, he was an insensitive helmsman and his experience was with powerful, brutal boats. Like Charley Morgan, he underestimated the role of the helmsman in sensing and achieving boat speed. The boat—design, shape, sails—was everything to him. He saw the helmsman as the key to tactics, not development.

But a twelve meter helmsman must be primarily a helmsman, not a tactician or anything else. The key to developing a Twelve to its potential is boat speed, "finding the groove" of optimum speed at any point of sailing. In developing sails and maneuvers, crew and advisors must get used to the way the helmsman steers. The sails must be cut and recut for the angle of heel and the attack angle at which the boat is taken to windward. A twelve meter hull is unlike any other. It is designed for a narrow range of conditions, moderate waves, winds under twenty-five knots. Its keel and control surfaces are minimized. The hull shape is a deep, full "V" that plunges with no pronounced bulges into the vestigial keel itself. When a Twelve heels in going to windward, she makes three to four degrees of leeway. Thus, although a helmsman can tack inside sixty-five degrees and keep his sails full, the best he can make good is between seventy and eighty degrees if he is sufficiently attentive to boat speed. Twelves are slow to respond to the helm. They don't flutter along and talk to your fingers like a dinghy. Heavy, they can be steered too close to the wind and still move at a good rate, slowing imperceptibly. But pinched, they make more leeway than usual, confuse sail trim and shape, and defeat their designer's intentions. To develop a Twelve's potential, a helmsman needs a tactician to watch the opposition, a navigator to estimate the course made good and call the

layline, a trimmer to manage the sails, and powerful folk on deck and winches. Along with these functionaries, he needs a coach to block out the moves that best relate the crew to the equipment. The helmsman's primary function is maximizing boat speed. To focus the helmsman's attention on anything else is to defeat development of sails and techniques.

A simple illustration will make this point clear. Charley Morgan, masterminding *Heritage*'s 1970 campaign, couldn't help observing everything. As a result his navigator learned that *Heritage* made good about eighty-four degrees from port tack to starboard tack with Morgan at the helm. Once, when Morgan gave the helm to Steve Colgate, the navigator estimated that Colgate might make good as little as seventy-eight degrees; but in fact he made good seventy-four degrees and *Heritage* overstood the mark. A ten-degree difference—five degrees on each tack—would require a different shape to the sails, different tactics, even different ballast.

Bond saw his role as coach, and as coach he made all hands compete for positions on the team; so, while everyone became expert, his boat was never tailored for a particular team, never developed to potential. He had a capable project supervisor in Brian Leary, a personable managerial type with sailing experience. The helmsmen on his two Twelves were Olympic champion John Cuneo and Jim Hardy, a proven helmsman but a "loser," and thus not Bond's leading candidate. Bond further complicated his decision-making process by signing on several sailmakers, several good tacticians, several good foredeck men, and many experienced hands. The two boats and the many hands sailed daily in the rambunctious waters off Yanchep Sun City, whose harbor and yacht club predated other amenities.

It is generally estimated that Bond's entire venture ran over $6,000,000. Even subtracting the carload of specially canned beer and the hand embroidered 12/KA4 neckties, there was more than enough money to design and campaign two Twelves. "Of all sad words of tongue or pen, the saddest are, 'It might have been.' " If Bond had given $2,000,000 to Alan Payne to design and campaign a Twelve, and spent the other $4,000,000 on Bob Miller's *Southern Cross*, what would the competition in Newport have generated? Had he chosen a helmsman as soon as Hardy and Cuneo raced together—and it was apparent that Hardy could move a boat to weather better than Cuneo—instead of waiting through six months of back-and-forth till late July, how much better would *Southern Cross* have sailed? If he had chosen his crew well in advance, how would they have improved the boat?

The situation in the U.S. looked great, though there remained several months of watchful waiting before it jelled. The *Mariner* syndicate managed to find itself a tax shelter and raised more than three-quarters of a million for openers. They were going ahead with plans to have Brit Chance design a new hull, *Mariner*, and redesign *Valiant*, providing their challenge with a controlled experiment.

The fortunes of war had brought two clients to Olin Stephens. Stephens had often murmured about a redesigned Twelve's being highly competitive. In 1967, the redesigned *Columbia*, rebuilt by Gerry Driscoll and sailed by Bill Ficker, was the finalist against the breakthrough *Intrepid*. Then *Intrepid*, reworked by Brit Chance, was the winner in Ficker's hands in her second incarnation. What was more natural than to have Driscoll rebuild *Intrepid* and make the next try for the defense of the Cup? At the same time, Stephens was designing *Courageous* for a New York Yacht Club syndicate headed at first by Bill Strawbridge and later managed by the troika of Briggs Dalzell, Bob McCullough and Joe Bartram. So S & S had two syndicates, headed by two groups of experienced men, competing with select crews and well-known skippers.

To make the S & S approach even stronger, Lowell North was emerging as a sailmaking rival for Ted Hood. Cooperating with Bainbridge to produce sailcloth, North captured championship after championship and market after market in the small classes, and began to dominate the One-Ton class. He acquired a young genius, John Marshall, who brought highly sophisticated computer techniques and original ideas into sailmaking. This combination itched to compete with Hood, who was sailmaker for *Courageous*. The competition could only help the S & S camp, which was in the pleasant position of having an East Coast and a West Coast boat, two sailmakers, two master helmsmen and two sets of tank tests from different tanks.

The dominance of the Davidson tank received a serious challenge from California, where a bigger tank at Lockheed was testing models on a larger scale. Experiments in towing full-sized boats proved that data scatter diminished sharply when models reached two or more inches to the foot. The California tank produced some ideas for the redesign of *Intrepid* which, checked in the Davidson tank, were adapted for *Courageous*.

Then the fuel crisis hit the United States, the stock market plunged into the six-hundreds, and men who had just had their millions halved were suddenly unavailable to fund raisers. While Bond, Miller, Hardy, and Cuneo sailed their Twelves at Yanchep Sun City, work halted on the *Courageous* project, and Bill Strawbridge asked the New York Yacht Club for a one-year postponement of the America's Cup, "in light of the energy crisis." He said that under the circumstances it "seemed inappropriate to hold a match."

From Yanchep Sun City, Alan Bond flared that postponement was a New York Yacht Club device "to keep the Cup." He had already stirred the pot and attempted to establish the NYYC in the "bad guys" role by declaring that his vast expenditure of money was the only way to combat American "space technology, 123 years of experience, and willingness to amend the rules." Bond's consistent response to the NYYC was to leave no turn unstoned, and the press loved it.

The New York Yacht Club takes the grace and gentility of its own image very seriously, and they denied Strawbridge's request before Bond could open his mouth, which he did anyway. They announced the races would be held as scheduled. In a firm, quiet, unpublic way, they conferred with the *Courageous* group and "encouraged" them to seek further funding. Ten days after Strawbridge's orders had gone out to stop work on *Courageous* they were rescinded.

Actually, the work had barely paused because Minneford's yard and the S & S office made a well-educated guess that nothing so minor as financial disaster and fuel crisis could cure Cup fever. One of the victims of *Courageous'* stagger in her long march to victory was Bill Ficker. He had made commitments to clients when the "cancellation" news hit; now, in order to honor his professional commitments, he had to pull out. His withdrawal put Strawbridge et al. in a sticky situation; "encouraged" to raise further funds, they had lost their leading man. Before Strawbridge could recover, tactician Steve Van Dyke and navigator Peter Wilson also pulled out. Shaken, Strawbridge passed the management of the syndicate into new hands, men who had not been as closely associated with fund raising for Twelves and were less dismayed than he by the prospect.

The new troika consisted of Briggs Dalzell, Joe Bartram and Bob McCullough. The circle widened, and fund raising and the *Courageous* campaign went ahead. Dalzell, a New York tugboat-magazine executive, is a magnificent organizer and prefers to work behind the scenes, where he can have a finger on everything. Joe Bartram is the red-headed opposite of Dalzell—gregarious and energetic, he moves with authority, and in his wake things happen. Bob McCullough was manager and skipper of the *Valiant* effort, had a three-Cup background, and had the knowledge and wisdom to work up the boat. With Dalzell in charge of the budget, Bartram managing the waterfront activities, and McCullough in charge of coaching and equipment, *Courageous* was once again on course, and all she needed was a crew.

Into this crisis—with some strong persuasion—stepped Bob Bavier. As winner of the America's Cup in *Constellation* and editor of *Yachting,* Bavier was the perfect name to attract funds. He had turned down the helm of *Intrepid* in 1967 with the plea that he was an older man and lacked recent experience in match racing. Nevertheless, he stepped into the breach, and assembled a crew that was easily the equal of *Intrepid/West*'s. His navigator was Halsey Herreshoff; with Dick McCurdy's computer, "Sidney

Greybox," as a sidekick, Herreshoff never overstood a mark or missed a windshift all summer. More than anyone else on the crew, his performance was consistently superior to that of his opposite number.

Bavier's tactician was Jack Sutphen, who, as a Ratsey man, was also a prime adviser on sail trim. Here, perhaps, two men would have been better. Sutphen, a gifted tactician, played an ambivalent role, and his tactical talents were not fully utilized so that Bavier could concentrate sufficiently on steering. Later, Hood came aboard as sailtrimmer and windward helmsman, and finally as helmsman. Dennis Conner, after *Mariner*'s demise, became starting helmsman and tactical advisor. The crew boss was Sam Wakeman, and Dave Pedrick, who had followed *Courageous* from tank through launching as design supervisor, came to Newport as project manager for S & S.

The *Mariner* campaign, off to an excellent managerial and financial start, ran into its own roadblocks. Chance had approached George Hinman with the idea of forming a syndicate, and asked for the right to veto Hinman's choice of helmsman. Denied this right, he nevertheless agreed to design a Twelve. Ted Turner, twice Yachtsman of the Year and World Ocean-Racing champion, was Hinman's choice. As owner and campaigner of *American Eagle* in the ocean-racing mode, Turner had experience with at least one Twelve. But he brought pretty much his own ocean-racing crew with him. Chance realized this during early crew conferences about deck layout and general responsibilities, and it diminished his confidence in Turner's ability to manage a slightly superior Twelve with winning finesse. So Chance set about designing a breakthrough Twelve which would win by itself. His tank tests took too long, and the lines were a month late. The builder, Bob Derecktor, worked at fever pitch, and the boat was finished only two weeks behind the original launch date, but it proved to be far from a "breakthrough." After abortive performances in the early Long Island Sound races, Chance was back at the drawing board and in the tank looking for a solution. By the end of a month of sail and crew development in Newport, *Mariner* convinced even Chance that the tank had betrayed him—that he had taken too big a step for the tank to handle. On June 28, *Mariner* and *Valiant* returned to Derecktor's for redesign and rebuild. *Valiant* went back to her S & S lines, with a sidelong glance at *Intrepid*, and the after-end of *Mariner* was dismantled as far forward as amidships while more tank tests were conducted. Finally Chance found a shape which pleased him. Hinman, once bitten and twice shy, called DeSaix and was reassured. Derecktor worked overtime—at $12.50 per hour per man plus materials—and *Mariner* was back in Newport thirty-eight days after she left.

A thirty-eight-day handicap out of a ninety-day season was too much, however, and *Mariner* never made it. Her helm was taken away from Turner for the final trials and turned over to Dennis Conner. With tactician Graham Hall, navigator Rich duMoulin, and sailtrimmer Robbie Doyle, Conner won most of his starts. He fought a good fight, but never found *Mariner's* true speed and lost all his races to *Intrepid* and

Courageous. Mariner, campaigned again, may yet show what Chance can do. Her failure is a sad tale, and demonstrates that designing a Twelve is like conducting a symphony: you can vary interpretation but you can't rewrite the score.

Out on the West Coast, the Intrepid III syndicate, sponsored by the Seattle Sailing Foundation, had an initial tax advantage over the NYYC–Courageous group, and for a while it looked as though all the advantages were flowing their way. With her light mast and highly developed sails, Intrepid would have fewer growing pains than the all-new Courageous. The evidence from the Lockheed towing tank, where eight-foot models were used, gave promise of increased reliability. George Schuchart of Seattle, George Jewett of San Francisco, and Charles Hughes guaranteed the necessary funds for her reconstruction.

The man charged with the task of rebuilding Intrepid was Gerry Driscoll, long-time friend of Olin Stephens. Like the others, Driscoll was exposed to yacht racing at an early age and had built a full life around it as builder, World Star

Class champion and Congressional Cup creator. When Olin Stephens redesigned Columbia, Driscoll rebuilt her in 1966 and helped make her a selection trials finalist in 1967. He also sailed as tactician on Valiant. In these previous campaigns Driscoll was beaten twice as defender of the America's Cup by Intrepid, and was therefore keen for the opportunity to work on her.

One of Intrepid's main advantages was time, and Driscoll made full use of it. Intrepid was trucked from City Island to his West Coast yard in the early fall of 1973, where Driscoll removed all of the changes made by Brit Chance and a few of the original sections. Just before he began work on the underbody, he got an additional break. The International Yacht Racing Union ruled that old framing on wood Twelves could be replaced with aluminum; as a result, Intrepid/West would turn out to be the lightest boat in Newport. Intrepid came out of Driscoll's yard in February 1974, more than three months before Courageous was launched, and her crew had two months to drill against Columbia before she had to be trucked east.

Driscoll's experience in *Valiant*'s defeat convinced him that compartmentalization of responsibility and refinement of technique were essential to achieve full potential. He built a crew around three key men: John Marshall, North sailmaker and Olympic bronze medalist; Bill Buchan, a World's Star champion and Congressional Cup winner; and Andy McGowan, who had been foredeck boss for *Intrepid*'s second campaign.

Marshall brought as much confidence to the *Intrepid/West* effort as Jack Kennedy had brought to the American presidency. A new era was dawning in which twelve meter sails developed rapidly. Marshall's ocean-racing sails, made in the North loft in North Stratford, Connecticut, were serious challengers to Hood's. Marshall's own enormous sincerity and firm belief in his own practices generated faith in the rest of the group. Marshall is a scholarly man of great talent who lives with a computer. The opportunity to spend an entire summer working on a single hull with a limited number of sails afforded him the sort of research laboratory every sailmaker

dreams about. Moreover, Marshall started with a fully developed set of America's Cup winning Hood sails against which to measure, analyze, and work.

Bill Buchan's qualifications in tactics and helmsmanship matched Driscoll's own. If the two could manage a gainful cooperation, they could learn *Intrepid*'s quirks and peculiarities together, and alternate the helm and tactician slots through the intense, draining afternoons of ultimate competition on the Newport course.

McGowan had a double advantage: he had been through the mill once, and he had beautiful hands in the mechanical sense. If it could be done, he could do it faster and better. His experience must have made him expensive to the *Intrepid/West* group. The first rule regarding America's Cup equipment is, "Renew early, and if there's any doubt, throw it out."

The only possible disadvantage the *Intrepid/ West* group had was that they were operating on a budget of some $500,000 less than *Courageous*'. *Intrepid* did not have some of the more sophisticated devices, and her navigator had no

complex computer with which to work. *Courageous'* headstay had twin grooves which enabled her to set one genoa inside another and change without ever losing drive; *Intrepid* had a steel rod headstay, and had to hank on one sail under another, drop the other, unclip it, and then run up the new sail. But there are drawbacks to complexity. Sails running up inside or outside one another are not good airfoil surfaces, and probably slow a boat down as much as a fifteen-second empty foretriangle. A sail on hanks drops instantly and allows the spinnaker to fill earlier; one in a groove must be pulled down against its own friction. Also, the hanked sail is less likely to slip overboard and cause drag. *Intrepid* did not have a hydraulic backstay-tension equalizer, but *Courageous* discarded hers in mid-season.

Intrepid's whole operation was low key. Her tenders and chase boats were lobsterman type; there was no large storage shed or shop in the Newport Shipyard. Instead, they had one trailer for sails and another for mechanical repairs, and a small office for public relations. Her backers had sixty-foot yachts at the Williams and Manchester dock, while the *Courageous* and *Mariner* yachts ran up to one hundred feet and were in their own name-labeled slips at the Newport Shipyard. *Intrepid*'s crews were housed in modest dwellings around Newport, with only one group in a place large enough for a cocktail party. *Courageous* had one of Newport's most elegant and famous mansions, "Hammersmith Farm," whose grounds extended half a mile from the road to the waterfront and were almost as wide as they were deep. The "Intrepids" bicycled from residence to dock. Their young wives were "gophers" and ran errands around town on their bikes. Day after day through the long summer and into the fall, the "Intrepids" alternately painted the bottom of their boat and sanded it down with #700 wet-or-dry by themselves.

Intrepid and *Courageous* arrived in Newport on the eleventh and twelfth of June, respectively, in characteristic style. *Intrepid* was trucked across the country via the southern route, and arrived thoroughly dried out, and with a few dings in her hull from stones cast up by passing traffic. She was launched at Branford, Connecticut, and towed to Newport with a minimal crew where she arrived with no fanfare and was immediately hoisted out of the water on *Heritage*'s hydraulic tripod. *Courageous* came up Long Island Sound from Oyster Bay in convoy, towed by Joe Bartram's *Exact*, with Bob McCullogh's *Inverness* riding wing. They sailed by Hammersmith Farm, and swung into the Hammersmith dock (the same one used in "The Great Gatsby"), where the Auchinclosses and the Dalzells ran up the green and white "26" Syndicate flag and fired a brass cannon made by Sidney Herreshoff, navigator Halsey's grandfather. *Inverness* responded by firing her signal cannon, which in turn brought a predictable response from all the available dogs and caused a small child to burst into tears. *Courageous* proceeded to the Newport Shipyard where a reception committee served dockside cheerers California champagne in plastic glasses, and appropriate speeches were made, full of hope and modesty.

The stage was set: East versus West; Hood versus North; wood versus aluminum; bicycles versus Mercedes Benz; and Sparkman & Stephens versus Sparkman & Stephens.

Chapter Eight
THE 1974 CAMPAIGNS:
Theory Becomes Practice

There are social rituals during an America's Cup Summer, in addition to the endless sailing drills. The crews are introduced to Newport society in an orderly succession of cocktail parties, receptions, and dances. Before the races begin, there is an English Speaking Union Ball, followed by a scatter of private parties and dances and the presentation of Rolex watches to the two final crews at a dinner dance. When the races are over, the Australians throw a beer-and-steak bash for the crews, the press, and their ladies.

The first party of 1974 was at Hammersmith Farm, at which the New York Yacht Club's sense of protocol was meticulously observed by the *Intrepid/West* group. They were carefully dressed in their official jackets and US/22 neckties; clearly, they had been instructed to conduct themselves in as low-key and un-Californian manner as possible. The younger crewmen tended to cluster around the prettier girls, while old hands busily greeted and socialized with Newporters they had met in years past. Reporters questioned skippers and syndicate members when they could get them clear of the Bellevue Avenue crowd (those who summer in Newport mansions). Trays of hors d'oeuvres circulated; a bar was set up at either end of the porch, overlooking the inlet beyond a green field in which five saddle horses grazed peaceably behind rail fences. The party began at 1800 and the sun lay long on the trees to the northeast. As Jamestown gradually darkened, the guests began to leave, drifting down through the trees across the dark lawns east of the house to where their cars were parked in a large field. It was early in the summer; everyone was subdued, and there was no singing.

The Observation Races began the end of June. The NYYC's first duty was to the *Mariner* syndicate; it took only four races to confirm the fact that *Mariner* had serious problems. So she left for Derecktor's yard and did not return for thirty-eight days. Then *Intrepid* and *Courageous* were pitted against one another. *Courageous* did very well during the early part of the week, but toward the end she lost two races to *Intrepid*. In the first one *Intrepid* was flattening her main by bowing her mast in twenty or more knots of air and was standing up better than *Courageous*. Where *Courageous'* main backwinded heavily, *Intrepid*'s was flat; she carried her genoa flatter than *Courageous* and sailed higher. *Intrepid* tried a small spinnaker on the final downwind leg, and *Courageous* tried a huge one whose shoulders kept folding. It cost her a minute and was never used again.

After the first race, the Committee sent them around again, this time on a four-leg windward-leeward course. *Courageous* used a different mainsail. Bavier won the start and sat on Driscoll's wind, demonstrating tactics and at the same time, he realized, contributing to Driscoll's wisdom. For whatever reason, he let Driscoll out from under cover and simply sailed *Courageous* for speed, tuning against *Intrepid*. *Intrepid* beat *Courageous* to the weather mark by twenty-three seconds, and gained three more seconds. The race fell apart when *Courageous* lost her spinnaker while taking it down, and carried it flogging to windward until she was able to winch it in. This cost her two more minutes. She lost the second round by more than three minutes.

The first week's races told Driscoll that *Courageous* could beat him in very light air; it told *Courageous* that *Intrepid* could win in more air, and that sail handling should be improved. There was now an interim period in which *Intrepid* would work on more draft in her sails for light air, and *Courageous* toward less draft in her heavy sails. Bavier thought all of *Courageous'* sails were cut too full. "Sailmakers always cut sails too full for Twelves," he said. "Even the genoas have too much draft. You know, once the genoas are flatter they won't throw so much air back into the main, and we'll have a different boat to weather."

Olin Stephens or Dave Pedrick apparently had a further thought, because early Monday morning the foam fill between *Courageous'* lead keel and her hull was dug out preparatory to putting more ballast aft of amidships. At the *Intrepid* dock there was talk of six new "second generation" sails for light air. On Wednesday, July 5, *Intrepid* and *Courageous* went out informally and raced with their altered sails. In ten-knot airs,

Intrepid led at the first windward mark by a boatlength. Both boats were also experimenting with different masts—*Courageous* with a new more sophisticated one, and *Intrepid* with her spare.

The second round of Observation Trials came a week later, and on Saturday, July 12, *Intrepid* and *Courageous* each won one race. In both races, *Courageous* could come down on *Intrepid* like a blanket if the wind was under twelve knots on the leeward legs. Tactically, each skipper won one race on downwind maneuverings—Bavier on aggressive guile, and Driscoll on evasive adroitness.

Fog, repairs after a collision between Turner on *Valiant* and Driscoll on *Intrepid,* and *Courageous'* loss of her backstay crane on the nineteenth backed the next confrontation off until July 20, when fluky airs told no one very much about the boats. Again, each won one race—or part of one, as the final race was called in mid-flight. The score was now tied four to four between the two S & S boats, and there were two days to go until the final Observation Races.

On July 23, Driscoll won the start. He luffed Bavier head to wind, fell off with boat speed and then sat on Bavier for the leg. Bavier carried a five-ounce Hood genoa and initiated a fifty-three-tack duel, getting as far as *Intrepid*'s windshadow and no farther. Going downwind, he whittled *Intrepid*'s fifty-seven-second advantage to twenty-seven seconds, went to a five-ounce Ratsey genoa, and sailed for fifteen minutes in perfect tune until he was close under *Intrepid,* only to be blocked again by her dirty air to the windward mark. He reached away from *Intrepid,* who ran straight off, and at one point he seemed to be ahead, but came back in the rather shifty air twenty-five seconds behind at the bottom mark. Now Bavier pitted his crew's endurance against *Intrepid*'s, and for fifty-nine tacks the huskies ground and the tailers handed flawlessly, but Driscoll drove Bavier off to leeward and back and finished with a lead of one minute.

Again and again, the trial races demonstrated that the two boats were absolutely equal, and the winner of the start was the winner of the race. This pattern held until the last trial, when Driscoll started behind and won, finishing the Observations with a score of *Intrepid* 6, *Courageous* 4. As they approached the windward mark, Driscoll's pressure forced Bavier to pinch a little, demonstrating that *Courageous* had to be driven full or she drifted off. A quarter mile from the mark, the one-length difference grew rapidly to a two-tack, forty-five-second gap, and from then on Driscoll maintained his lead. *Intrepid*'s new downwind technique was to let the backstays go entirely, bend her titanium-topped mast forward over the bow by taking up on the jib halyard, thus carrying her headstay, which has about eight thousand pounds tension on the wind, with a catenary sag like the support wires of the Newport Bridge. *Intrepid* was now going very well, and she won the Caritas and Astor Cups on the New York Yacht Club Cruise, both in decent breezes.

As late as August, with *Intrepid* holding a slight edge, *Courageous* continued to conduct endless sailtrimming drills. It was August 2; the morning calm had died and the wind filled in from the southwest at fifteen knots, when Lee Van Gemert arrived from Marblehead with two genoas—a recut one and a new heavy one. They were loaded aboard the chase boat, *Escort*, and delivered to *Courageous* out by the Cup buoy. Those aboard *Escort* included Olin Stephens, Sam Wakeman, and Chris Wick. As the first sail went up, it looked too full and *Escort* suggested it be "taken up a little higher." It looked better, but *Escort* thought there was still "too much bucketing in the leach."

Escort to *Courageous*: "Chris, what tension do you have on the mast?"

Courageous: "It's at four, with no backstay."

Escort: "Don't take it on the leach of the mainsail; take it on the backstay."

Courageous' headstay was flat oval in section, and each edge had a slit running up it, hollowed to a tube inside the slit. Her sail went up in the slit, held in because it was sewn around a rope which was a little smaller than the hollow but bigger than the slit. With one sail up, she could run another sail up in the other slit and then pull down the original, so that her foretriangle was never empty. However, the friction of the groove kept the sail from dropping and made hoisting slower.

The genoa looked a little better and so did the main. The Narragansett shore was getting in the way, so *Courageous* tacked and both the genoa and the main looked a little better on the other side. Stephens decided to go aboard *Courageous* for a bit. *Escort* eased alongside at about eleven knots, Stephens stepped across and *Escort* sheered away. The second genoa still needed to be checked, and *Valiant* was in the area. *Courageous* waited to observe the effect of the change until she was sailing even with *Valiant.*

Courageous to *Escort:* "We're in the starboard groove on the center halyard, so we'll be going up in the port groove on the port halyard. . . . It's up and we're just taking up the last on the halyard."

Escort: "It looks pretty good, a little less bucketing in the leach than the other sail. It looks better than anything we've seen so far. If your halyard is now reading two from max, I think

seriously you should re-mark the halyard—it looks at least six."

Now the work doubled. A starting line was set up; after three starts, the two boats raced twice around a one-mile triangle to observe sail changes. Wakeman coached the manipulators, and they continued to chatter about sails.

Even with a computer, sailtrimming is less than an exact science. The tension on the luff of a genoa can be altered by halyard tension, backstay tension or boarding down the mainsail. Since the halyards stretch, benchmarks which translate observational description into scientific computation have only relative and fleeting validity.

On August 3, *Courageous* was underway at 0930. The fog in the harbor was so thick she had to be towed out on a compass course. Just north of Newport Bridge it was clear, and *Courageous* spent two hours in the area sailing in circles. At noon, *Intrepid* got underway and headed toward Newport Bridge, passing *Courageous* under the arches. She went somewhat below the Navy base, chose two Navy anchoring buoys as top and bottom marks, and set up her chase boat as wing mark. The distance between marks was less than half a mile. *Intrepid* then sailed a complete America's Cup course six times—36 legs, 150 maneuvers—tacking, jibeing, setting, striking, and timing.

The purpose of the exercise, according to George Schuchart, the coach, and "Sunny" Vynne, the timer, was to get the optimum time for a tack. With a steady wind, they measured the distance and time from the start of a tack until the boat was sheeted home and in top tune. The object was to defeat *Courageous* in a tacking duel. Two days earlier, Bavier had made ground on them throughout two windward legs in tacking duels, and they noticed that he was taking about thirteen seconds from full to full, while *Intrepid* was making it in ten seconds. Tacking this fast, they lost distance by not carrying their windward momentum into the tack. Marshall signalled when trim and speed had optimized, and they determined that about fifteen seconds was the ideal tempo. From a forward position, Marshall could tension the backstays, the boom

out-thrust, and adjust the Cunningham tension, and thus control the shape of the mainsail without having to relay orders to cockpit or coachpit. Earlier in the season, only *Intrepid* did this, but eventually *Courageous* and *Southern Cross* followed suit.

Once they decided tacking tempo, they concentrated on spinnaker jibeing. The foredeck man had been standing forward on the headstay with both arms reaching inside. As the pole was dipped through the foretriangle, he unsnapped the old guy and snapped in the lazy guy. The idea occurred that he might stand inside the headstay with his back braced against it, thus putting his weight slightly out of the bow. Four attempts pleased no one, particularly the pole manipulators, and the idea was scrubbed.

At 1630 *Intrepid* headed back to Williams and Manchester's and was hauled onto her A-frame. The crew gathered around Driscoll in the cockpit, and Paul Coble, the project engineer, climbed the staging with his notebook. George Schuchart climbed into the cockpit with his notes, and for about twenty minutes they exchanged comments and criticisms while reporters, wives, and syndicate members chatted idly on the dock.

Before the preliminary selection trials were scheduled to begin, *Courageous* was visited with a lovely piece of good luck. Ted Hood had shipped his one-tonner to Europe for the World Championships, and it had gotten caught in a shipping strike. Unable to retrieve it and sail in the World's, Hood was unexpectedly available for the Cup races. Bavier immediately signed him on as opposite number to John Marshall.

Marshall was full of his "second generation sails." *Intrepid*'s North sails were cut to the same basic design as her successful, but worn, Hoods, then further refined until they looked perfect. "But," said Marshall, "a cosmetically perfect sail doesn't necessarily move the boat perfectly. We have a performance recorder aboard that relates wind speed, boat speed, and angle of attack. I take the tape home to my computer to check it with previous performances in the computer's memory bank. You begin to get indications of how to design a better sail. What we're working

on now is smoother flow."

Marshall made his new sails by welding together two layers of finely woven sailcloth, which produced a slicker surface and more consistent elasticity.

The first selection trial was held August 15; *Intrepid* won, but she sailed against a faster *Courageous*. Driscoll won the start and rounded the top mark with a thirty-seven-second lead. *Courageous* gained on her toward the wing mark, but inexplicably went wind-hunting and rounded the wing mark 1:32 back. Pitting a starcut spinnaker against a reaching jib, *Courageous* took back twenty-five seconds. Then, with Hood at the helm and aided by a windshift two hundred yards below the windward mark, she rounded fifteen seconds in the lead. Downwind, *Intrepid*'s wind shadow reached her, and *Intrepid* stole a little as she jibed flawlessly every three minutes down the leg while *Courageous* jibed out from under. *Courageous*' jibes were a trifle ragged, and the attrition showed as she rounded only eight seconds in the lead. Both boats split tacks, and *Intrepid* powered into the clear when *Courageous* dropped her spinnaker in the water. She was at least a minute behind when she recovered, and managed to take back only twenty-nine seconds on the windward leg.

Intrepid lost the next race. The start was even—both boats stalled at the line and broke away on opposite tacks. There was no duel, just the "Virginia Reel" cover where the opponents tack out and back from each other, neither with enough advantage to bother the other. At the mark, *Intrepid* led by eighteen seconds. Neither gained on the reaching legs. On the next windward leg, *Intrepid* gained twenty-two seconds and appeared to have made hay; but now *Courageous* laid a little wind shadow on *Intrepid,* and jibe by jibe, she took back all but twelve seconds. At the bottom mark, *Intrepid*'s spinnaker halyard jammed. She tacked on *Courageous* and blanketed her for a minute or so, got her bag down and was moving again, but *Courageous* had broken *Intrepid*'s cover and had perhaps a ten-second advantage. Going up the leg, they did the "Virginia Reel" again, and *Courageous*' lead diminished. In the last pair of tacks, *Courageous* pinched to keep *Intrepid* to leeward; Driscoll drove off for speed to get through while he was free and almost made it. They came to the finish line on opposite tacks and *Courageous* won by *two seconds.*

Apparently Marshall's faith in his second generation sails was justified—they might just prove to be tie-breakers. Someone in the *Courageous* syndicate panicked and ordered a second generation mainsail. Marshall pointed out that a sailmaker's commitment is to do his best for every client. On August 21, *Courageous* beat *Intrepid* decisively, with both boats setting North mainsails. Hood handled *Courageous* on the weather legs. The wind averaged 4.5 knots—and *Intrepid*'s weakness was in light air.

On August 23, *Courageous* was leading in two trial races when the Committee called them for windshifts. Then one of the great races of all time was sailed on the twenty-fifth.

Mariner had been retired by the Selection Committee, and her superb reservoir of talent leaked onto *Intrepid* and *Courageous*. Rich duMoulin, her navigator, came aboard *Intrepid* for that slot, and Dennis Conner, who had replaced Ted Turner as skipper of *Mariner*, stepped onto his third Twelve of the summer as *Courageous'* starting helmsman, a spot he would henceforward fill with entertaining originality. In addition, a package of new *Mariner* sails, including a Ratsey reaching spinnaker and a third generation North main, was delivered to *Courageous.*

On August 25, Conner circled with *Intrepid* about five hundred yards from the line; about thirty seconds before the gun, with *Intrepid* in the controlling position astern of *Courageous,* *Intrepid* broke for the line as Conner tacked and filled. Then, as *Intrepid* gathered way, Conner tacked on her, blanketed her, and went for the line. When the gun went off, both boats were two hundred feet back, but *Courageous* crossed thirty-two seconds before *Intrepid,* virtually the largest lead she was to have throughout the race. Conner handed the helm to Bavier, and, not surprisingly, Bavier did not get into tune quite as soon as *Intrepid*. *Intrepid* worked up parallel with *Courageous,* but couldn't break through her

cover. They rounded the weather mark seventeen seconds apart.

On the reaching leg, *Intrepid* reached across *Courageous'* stern, got upwind of her, sailed through her, took her wind, and jibed into clear air. The Hood–Bavier–Conner tactical troika lost that one by virtue of committee indecision, jibing too late. *Courageous* then drove down toward *Intrepid,* holding port until the last minute, then jibing onto starboard as *Intrepid* luffed up to a reach. *Courageous* sailed over her for the mark, and rounded, two jibes later, thirteen seconds in the lead. Cheers from the thirty or forty spectator boats would have done justice to a high school football championship.

As they rounded the wing mark, *Intrepid* reached across *Courageous'* stern, well to weather of her, hoping to avoid tactics and simply outsail her to the bottom mark. *Courageous* ran straight for the mark, her mast hooked over her bow, her course arrow-straight. Both boats set highcut staysails inside their spinnakers. *Intrepid* slowly ate away at *Courageous'* lead until, with an overlap and inside *Courageous,* it looked as though Driscoll could call for buoy room at the mark and start with a lead on the weather leg.

Courageous hoisted her genoa early and appeared to have trouble getting her spinnaker down. Then suddenly she snatched her spinnaker in, luffed *Intrepid* the wrong side of the mark while *Intrepid* fought a backwinded spinnaker, jibed under her, and scooted around the mark some twenty seconds ahead. *Intrepid* hoisted a protest flag, recovered her bag, initiated a tacking duel on the windward leg, and dropped to forty-seven seconds behind as the wind went lighter and *Courageous* methodically laid backwind upon her.

On the square leg, both boats reached apart—a navigator's tactic. At one point 1.5 miles separated them. When they came together at the bottom, the sun was on the horizon and *Courageous* had a fifteen-second lead. In very light air, *Courageous* got hooked up well and opened out about one hundred yards before *Intrepid* found her groove. The wind went around to southeast, both boats set reachers, and the setting sun showed *Intrepid*'s shadow slowly crossing *Courageous*' sails.

The wind went farther east; both set quarter-ounce spinnakers. Four hundred yards from the finish, *Courageous* got *Intrepid*'s wind, dumped *Intrepid*'s floater, and passed her. *Intrepid* shifted to a reacher, reached across *Courageous*' stern, set a spinnaker, took *Courageous*' wind, and forced *Courageous* to jibe away from the mark. As *Intrepid* passed her, *Courageous* jibed back, took *Intrepid*'s wind, reached over her, and slid slowly across the line, less than a boatlength ahead, the winner by ten seconds.

It was a masterpiece of match racing, flawless timing, and lovely luck, and it told the Selection Committee that both boats were tactically remarkable and remarkably equal in light air.

It told Alan Bond, who had now beaten *France* twice in their selection series, that the tactical situation he would encounter next was as superior to the present one as he believed his boat to be superior to the Americans'. Packer-style, he immediately prepared legal ground for himself by publicly deploring Conner's "cowboy" starting tactics.

The Americans raced again on the twenty-seventh. *Intrepid* had practiced with a new "third generation" mainsail and brought it to the line with only minor adjustments. It appeared to be the perfect sail, smooth of surface and steady of shape as a casting. The race was to speed, not tactics. Conner won the start, crossing behind *Intrepid* but with greatly superior boat speed. *Intrepid* did the "Virginia Reel" to the west to try for lifts, returning until *Courageous* was ahead of her, then going back west. Twenty-eight minutes after the start, after double-tacking thirteen times, *Intrepid* was on port tack, and was far enough ahead so that *Courageous* tacked under her. From there on *Intrepid* led by 0:15, 0:18, 0:40, 0:33, and 1:12 at successive marks. The wind blew ten to eighteen knots, more like the usual September velocity. *Courageous* had a problem in fresher airs, and two sails went off for recutting.

On the twenty-eighth, *France* lost for the fourth time—each time by a narrower margin than the last—and *Intrepid* won again. She won the start, let *Courageous* get ahead on a

windshift, and then on three windward legs in fifteen knots of air and a left-over lumpy sea she did the out-west-and-back pattern that had worked on the twenty-seventh, slowly eroding *Courageous*' lead until she rounded twenty-one seconds ahead. She led all the way, by sixteen, nineteen, thirty-one, thirty-eight, and finally fifty-two seconds. After the race, Driscoll commented on *Courageous*' four opening wins in the selection series. "You will notice," he said, "that they were all in very light air, and that we were highly competitive there, too." The implication was clear: What are they waiting for?

On August 30, and again on August 31, *Intrepid* led *Courageous* when the race ended, once at the finish line, and next as shifting winds and rainsqualls caused a hasty cancellation. The two races proved that if *Intrepid* was allowed to do her wind-hunting, west-seeking "Virginia Reel," she might luck onto a shift, then abandon the wind-hunt and sit on *Courageous*. *Courageous* was well aware of this, and on August 31, she took the start with the same tactic that had fooled Driscoll before—outstall him, get going from astern with more room, and then take his wind at the start. Then he stayed with *Intrepid* and rounded the weather mark fifty seconds ahead in fairly brisk air. The rest of the race was meaningless. Forty-degree windshifts preceded a front and eventually the race was called.

With five days left to run, the score was officially four to four. The equality of the boats in light air was clear, but a test of superiority in heavy weather was yet to come. The only proof that mattered to the Selection Committee, which wisely continued the series to the last moment, was current proof—not the New York Yacht Club Cruise or any other past history. They felt that the intense competition of the final trials had tuned both boats and crews to a pitch of competitive intensity that made previous performance irrelevant.

There was a growing feeling in the *Courageous* syndicate, however, that there were too many people in the cockpit for *Courageous* to respond reflexively to tactical problems. Hood had ten years of continuous experience and was a better windward helmsman than Bavier, who had re-

turned to the wars from more intermittent competition. Time passed while the syndicate weighed this consideration and turned to Bob McCullough for advice.

Then, after a layday, the Committee lost two days of possible racing to absolute calms. The fleet went out in golden, hazy sunlight, lay around while bathers dipped off spectator craft for two or three hours, cancelled and came in. Now only one day remained before the rules of the contest required a choice. The night before, McCullough and Bavier discussed the situation, and Bavier, reasonable and considerate as always, thought he should give the helm to Hood and see if this last, positive simplification would make the critical difference.

Courageous won the last possible selection race on the last possible selection day in authoritative style and with ironic touches.

The wind blew twenty-five to thirty knots— perhaps a little hard for an actual America's Cup start. Hood took the helm for the entire race. Knowing that *Courageous* was a bit more tender than *Intrepid,* he used a nine-ounce genoa with a

hollow leach and an old *Intrepid* heavy mainsail. Hood's Marblehead loft had made it for *Intrepid's* second defense, but Ficker hadn't liked it, and after recutting it, Hood had stored it against the time when another Twelve might need it. It was not a maximum area sail, and was ideal for the day.

Both boats went for the start at opposite ends of the line. Driscoll's timing was a trifle better; he crossed seven seconds ahead of Hood, but he had to tack to cover Hood and gave up six or seven seconds. Both boats now had their wind clear.

Intrepid initially had boat speed, and worked ahead but to leeward of *Courageous. Courageous* held and improved her weather gauge, and was lifted about twenty degrees by a windshift as they beat toward the Rhode Island shore in the rainy northeaster and got downwind of the Sakonnet River wind-funnel. Up to this point, Hood had been sailing with his mainsail flattened amidships. Now, as the wind increased, he let it off a bit wide on the traveler, took it up bar-hard on the leach by boarding down the sheet, and let

220

both leaches spill wind clean. *Courageous* stood up a few more degrees and took off. She rounded the weather mark forty-six seconds ahead of *Intrepid,* and started on a close reach for the wing mark, sheets freed, with the same sails.

Intrepid had broken a runner backstay halfway up the first leg, and for this leg she couldn't bend her mast properly on both tacks. This was her first gear failure of the summer, other than collision damage, but she was game, and to make up for lost time, she set a close reaching spinnaker under her genoa, dropped the genoa, and blew the spinnaker out of its luffropes. This cost her a few seconds, and she rounded the wing mark fifty-six seconds back. On the next reaching leg both boats set spinnakers, staysails under, and as they went down to the bottom mark, Andy McGowan went aloft and repaired the backstay. *Courageous* sailed this leg cautiously, holding to weather of *Intrepid* and taking down her spinnaker well before the mark. *Intrepid* held hers to the last possible second, snatched it down flawlessly, and rounded thirty-nine seconds behind, having picked up seventeen seconds on the leg.

Again, *Courageous* sailed defensively on the second weather leg. She engaged in a tacking duel with *Intrepid* and sat on her, tack for tack, never letting *Intrepid* out of phase. She rounded the weather mark forty-three seconds ahead. On the square run, both boats set spinnakers and drove straight down the course. *Courageous* took back seventeen seconds. Only the final leg remained for Hood to prove that *Courageous* was actually faster in strong winds than *Intrepid.* He concentrated on boat speed and ignored *Intrepid* entirely, gaining an additional forty-eight seconds. He commented after the race, "With the leftover southwest swell and the short new northeast seas, it was pretty hard to find her groove, but she went well in the last leg."

The Committee was satisfied, (and a bit relieved—if *Intrepid* was the ultimate Twelve, how soon would all challengers have ultimate Twelves? If you keep choosing the old boat for the defense, who will build a new one?) and made the ritual trip to *Intrepid*'s dock to thank them. It was a sad day for *Intrepid/West.* They had been so sure that they were superior in hard

winds that a victory banquet had been laid on for the evening. Even after the axe fell, they weren't really sure they couldn't have done it but for that backstay. It had been so close.

The formula had worked, and America had a defender whose capabilities were thoroughly known, whose growth had been continuous, whose experiments were over. Tried in relentless competition against an improving opponent, she had refined every technique to a certainty and developed an after-guard that could choose the exact moment for the exact tactic. Hood and Conner together had made plain that timing is everything, and that the emergency measure never pays. For the third time, one S & S Twelve with a superior crew had developed another S & S Twelve to peak. Stephens was present throughout the final pressures of the trials, observing, consulting with Bavier, with Hood, with Driscoll, with Marshall, with Pederick, with Covell, and letting the polished facts of competition suggest intuitions and fill the well for future designs.

Chapter Nine
SOUTHERN CROSS VS. COURAGEOUS:
The Product and the Prediction

Alan Bond is exceptionally astute. The final races between *Intrepid* and *Courageous* must have given him exceptional misgivings. His chosen helmsman, Jim Hardy, had defeated an *Intrepid*—in two races out of five—whose selection as defender was won in a low-key series. *Valiant* had offered no such competitive intensity as *Intrepid/West; Intrepid II*'s crew had been no more experienced than Hardy's. *Gretel II* and *Intrepid II* came as near-equals to the line. In 1974, despite a summer's tuning, *Southern Cross* was at a competitive disadvantage. With the Americans at the end of their experiments, Bond was still cutting and trying to find the keys to performance. On the fourth of September, reshaped, and with forty pounds less in rod rigging, swinging spreaders and a rotating base a remodeled mast was stepped in the *Cross*. The Australians went out and ran up all twelve of the sails they had now fairly well settled on.

That evening two Australians somehow got aboard *Courageous* and were detected *in flagrante*. . . . Next day the International Technical Committee was called to examine *Coura-*

geous' twin genoa winch-heads, which were recessed in the deck and cross-linked below deck. The Committee had been supplied with an 8 x 10 glossy photograph of the area, and a question from the Australian camp as to whether this "depression" was allowable under Rule 21, which reads:

Decks shall not have negative camber . . . (note: Small depressions used to accommodate particular and individual items, such as spinnaker booms, shall be permitted, provided that the method of construction, as approved by Lloyd's Register . . . retaining not less than the weight of the deck structure replaced by the recess. . . .).

After due deliberation, Sir Gordon Smith, James McGruer, and Bob Blumenstock agreed that the cross-linked drums were "an item," and that the depression, measuring some fourteen square feet, was smaller than the eighteen square feet of spinnaker pole depression, and thus could be allowed along with the latter. Bond's aim in raising the protest had been, of course, to force a slight change in the deck layout and a hangup in

the unvaried routine of the sheet handlers. Bond's next discovery was amusing—the IYRU allows only one window in a jib, and the Australian protest of *Courageous'* jibs resulted in the extra windows being sprayed white. Then the Aussie jibs were inspected, and—you guessed it—they had to have their extra windows opaqued.

Not in the least put off their stride by these bits of gamesmanship, *Courageous* came to the starting line of the first race on a hazy tenth of September 1974. Visibility was less than a mile, setting navigators in a tacking duel a real challenge—too much of a one, as it turned out, for Ron Packer and *Southern Cross*. The race finally started after two hours of postponements. While they waited, Conner and Hood alternated at the helm to get the feel of the day, and toured the spectator fleet garnering good wishes.

At 1400 the preliminary gun went. The wind was southwest at ten knots. Conner's start was a bit of ridiculous improvisation. He got on Hardy's stern, rode him to the line, and then had the next decision turned over to him, as Hardy stalled. Conner broke off and sailed for the buoy end of the line, with *Southern Cross* on his tail. When *Courageous* reached the America's Cup buoy, behind which the spectator fleet massed, he casually sailed into the fleet, abruptly went around the bow of the press boat, *Hel-Cat*, and wiped *Southern Cross* off. When *Courageous* came out from behind *Hel-Cat*, she was on Hardy's stern again, and they went again to the line, where Hardy, stalling, said in effect, "Over to you, Dennis."

Conner squeezed *Southern Cross* gently toward the Committee Boat, and when he had her more than one hundred yards from the favored buoy end of the line, he fell off on starboard tack toward the buoy. The *Cross*, to avoid being swept over the line on starboard tack, went through the wind and fell off to port. She had to dip the line and come back, so that when the gun went off, Conner was exactly at the buoy. He had good boat speed and shot across with the gun in commanding position with a fifteen-second advantage. After two minutes he tacked to port, and the race began with *Courageous* one hundred yards to weather of *Southern Cross* and perhaps thirty feet behind her. To let her get to leeward was a mistake.

The next half hour was all *Southern Cross*'s. Relentlessly, the *Cross* ate out from under *Courageous* and worked into the lead. Without tacking and without tactics, both boats approached the layline and the fringe of spectators, and *Southern Cross* tacked. Before she could cross ahead of *Courageous* and give her backwind, *Courageous* tacked under her in the safe leeward position. The wind dropped and began a gradual westward swing of about twelve degrees, putting *Courageous* on the wrong side of the round-up. Still slightly ahead, but now well to leeward of Hardy, Hood slowly squeezed up and forced Hardy to sail high of the mark.

Under these circumstances, the second the weather navigator knew he was high of the mark, he should have advised the helmsman to drive off and down on the leeward boat and give her bad air. Instead, the *Cross* continued to sail high, and Hood continued to squeeze up until both boats were substantially past the layline.

226

The *Courageous* suddenly swung down from her starboard tack to a close starboard reach, at least twelve degrees off the wind, and the *Cross*, astern now by the distance *Courageous* had been to leeward, was in *Courageous*' dirty air. In the last four minutes of running to the mark, *Southern Cross* lost at least ten seconds, and the boats rounded thirty-four seconds apart.

The windshift had converted the first reach into a square run, and *Courageous* set a new North quarter-ounce red-white-and-blue spinnaker, a gossamer-light floater. It was the perfect sail, and it forced the Australians into the second tactical error of the day. In the damp, foggy air, *Cross* set a larger half-ounce spinnaker, which wallowed and undulated and confused its own airflow. It cost them a minute by the wing mark, where she set a floater and lost eleven seconds going to the bottom. From then on it was a procession, 3:40 at the weather mark, 4:05 at the bottom, and 4:54 at the finish.

The first race in a match racing series is one where the opponents learn the nature of the competition. The Bond–Hardy team should have learned at least two things. First, their boat was faster to windward at twenty-five degrees to the apparent wind, but not at twenty-two. Second, their navigator needed to be more aware of his problems. Possibly a third idea might have occurred to them—that a trailing boat doesn't have to set a sail that is different from a leading boat's. The patience to make gains slowly, to time the key effort at the key moment, to make the all-or-nothing effort only at the last ditch requires confidence.

The Americans plainly knew that squeezing their opponent from leeward was the key to winning windward tactics. They may have concluded that in hazy weather, the Aussie navigator could find the mark only if the Americans rounded it first. They probably felt that *Southern Cross* tended to panic into extreme measures when behind.

Southern Cross lost the second race by only seventy-one seconds, and her second performance raised as many questions as her first. The start showed that neither Conner nor Hood wanted the *Cross* initially to leeward and free to drive off for speed. At the start, Hardy was behind and to windward of Conner, and fell off and ran the line toward the Committee Boat. Conner did the same, and crossed the line perhaps two seconds behind Hardy, both boats with their wind free. Conner tacked and handed the helm over to Hood; Hardy tacked to cover, and Hood began to squeeze *Courageous* up under *Southern Cross*. *Cross* tacked, encountered a windshift, and tacked back. As she approached *Courageous*, *Courageous* tacked on top of her and ahead. With minor windshifts of about five degrees the boats "Virginia-Reeled" for two more tacks, *Courageous* retaining a slight lead. But on the fourth rejoining, the *Cross* had found her groove and managed to cross ahead of *Courageous* by less than ten feet. Had she attempted to tack on top of *Courageous*, the tacking time would have put her behind, so she continued on a southerly, starboard tack. This was exactly the direction *Intrepid* had learned to avoid in her "Virginia Reel" cover of *Courageous*. The favoring lifts come in from the west and it is well to stay west of the rhumb line. When the boats were separated by a half-mile, *Courageous* (to the west) got a great lift, and *Southern Cross* a great knock. Newport photographer John Hopf, who was flying over the race, said that for more than three minutes *Southern Cross* was sailing at right angles to the mark and *Courageous* was laying it. The *Cross*, inexplicably, did not tack to the header.

The helmsman in a Twelve is not looking at a compass. He is to leeward, with his whole horizon blanked out by a deck-sweeping genoa, concentrating on the yarns that indicate air flow over the sails, on the sense of the helm, and on the instruments that record his speed. He must get the compass information from the navigator, and it must be passed through the tactician who analyzes the situation. Somewhere, in this chain of information on *Southern Cross,* there was a tenuous link.

The *Cross,* to windward of *Courageous* and not free to sail, made ground to the mark and rounded thirty-four seconds astern.

Cross gained on both reaching legs, setting the same sails as *Courageous;* at the wing mark she was twenty-six seconds behind and gained toward the bottom mark until she began to get *Courageous'* wind. But *Courageous* subtly squeezed to weather, carrying above the course to the mark, ran her wind clear, and headed again for the mark. The *Cross* had sailed too high too long and had to make a slow square run for the mark. In so doing she converted her faster downwind speed into a no-gain pair of legs, rounding still thirty-four seconds back.

On the square run from the second rounding of the windward mark, *Southern Cross* gained visibly at first, but the wind died down as the boats approached the shore, and the *Cross* gained only eleven seconds, rounding forty-five seconds back. (On the next windward leg, the *Cross* stuck close to *Courageous* and lost only twenty-two seconds, despite tacking four times more than *Courageous* and thus sacrificing at least twenty-two seconds in tacks.)

Sailing the final leg substantially alone, the *Cross* took long tacks to the west away from *Courageous* and then back toward her and dropped twenty-six more seconds.

Southern Cross and Hardy had improved their performance on the first race, but were still working with inadequate navigational savvy and insensitive tactics. It might be cruel to say that *Southern Cross* was only sailed well when she was close enough to take her cues from *Courageous*. To go a step further, it is possible that training with a "trial horse" builds a dependency, that only training with a real competitor forces a skipper and crew to lead, to initiate, to create tactics, and to explore possibilities. By the end of the second race, one had the feeling that a summer of training against a boat that had been "kept the same so we could see how much we had gained" had bred a dependence. For example, *Intrepid/West* had been beaten in tacks by *Courageous* until she retimed her tacking techniques and shot to windward longer during them. To the end of the America's Cup races, *Southern Cross* was slammed through tacks in less time than *Courageous*. *Gretel II*, of course, had to be tacked to full drive as rapidly as possible because she was still rather fully bustled. And how could *Southern Cross*, winning tacking duels

229

against *Gretel II*, know that she still had seconds to gain?

For the third race, Bond changed Packer for Jack Baxter as navigator, and Hugh Treharne for John Cuneo as tactician. But the pattern was as before. Hardy won a start by eight seconds, but windshifts and an eventual complete failure of the breeze allowed the time limit to run out.

The next start showed Conner at his most outrageous. With forty seconds to go, Conner moved from astern and to leeward of *Southern Cross,* and fell off on starboard for the buoy end of the line. He was early, so he let his jib flap, slowed, and, as the *Cross* fell off toward him, sheeted in and ran the line, blanketing the buoy from the *Cross's* vision. Then he sharpened and drove across the line at least three seconds early, carrying the *Cross* with him. Once across, he tacked behind Hardy, dipped the line, and passed between Hardy and the Committee Boat, preventing the Aussies from seeing that both the K4 and the "26" plaques were flipped on *Carltina* to indicate that both boats were early. By the time *Southern Cross* had the start sorted out,

Courageous was well to weather and sixteen seconds ahead.

The first leg was highly competitive, nonetheless, and, as usual, *Southern Cross* managed to get ahead of *Courageous,* who was forced to tack under her in the safe, leeward position. But a pair of windshifts and a strong current at the mark cost Hardy his advantagge, and he rounded forty-five seconds back. From here in, steadily failing air turned the race into a runaway, and *Courageous* won by 5:27.

The last race was a disaster. The Australians pushed the panic button, used a Kevlar main they hadn't practiced with for a month, and finished better than seven minutes back. Bob Miller, *Southern Cross's* designer, won the press pool on the finishing time with an estimate of sevenminutes and 15 seconds. Asked why, he said, "Well, they gave up racing yesterday and finished five back, so I started there; I added a minute for the Kevlar main, and threw in a minute for being farther behind and taking longer shots." So a good boat and spare-no-expense preparation had fallen through the triple holes of late selection of crew, lack of competitive racing, and, in the last races, a managed skipper.

In contrast to the decorous gathering on the lawns and porches of Hammersmith Farm that had begun the summer of the Twelves, the last party of the summer was uproarious. Whisky and rum were there for the asking, but everyone seemed bent on drinking the last of the *Southern Cross* beer, canned in Australia by Courage with the *Southern Cross* pictured on each can. The Australian base, "Chastellux," stands on a hill south of the Ida Lewis Yacht Club and overlooks the harbor, the lighted arcs of the Newport Bridge, and the dark bay surmounted by the sky-glow of Providence. The singing began as soon as the sun sank. Steaks sizzled on the grill while guests drank deep and chomped on huge bowls of potato chips, rolls, salad, crackers, and cheese. Candles flickered here and there, and the terrace was engulfed in a roar of voices, some singing, some just roaring, and all circulating madly. Late in the evening the grand spoof began, and the Press unearthed a hideous urn made of silvered plaster, which vaguely resembled the America's Cup. It was solemnly presented to Alan Bond, to be bolted to the floor at the Royal Perth, "until he gets the other, so the bolt won't get rusty." Bond countered with a speech in which he invited the reporters to tell the world that he would host a series of twelve meter match races at Yanchep Sun City, and would put everybody up. All they had to do was get their boats there, "and it'll be great practice and great experience for when they'll have to come down and get the real one back." Loud cheers, farewells, and a walk down the long entrance drive to the Newport waterfront by the silent Ida Lewis Yacht Club. There the six parking places painted with the names of the NYYC Race Committee stood empty in the moonlight.

Now, in 1977, a new challenge and a new defense is building. The American defense, tax-sheltered, pits the Maritime College at Fort Schuyler against the Merchant Marine Academy at Kings Point. The Fort Schuyler Foundation is sponsoring a new Sparkman & Stephens Twelve called *Enterprise*. She will be sailed by Lowell North, World's One-Ton champion, Olympic medalist, World's Star champion, winner of the Congressional Cup, and so on. Her crew will be, substantially, *Intrepid/West*'s crew: Andy McGowan, John Marshall, Rich DuMoulin, Steve Taft, Jim Caldwell, Bob Norman, Greg Gillette, and others.

The other Twelve, already launched in July 1976, put a summer of practice under her keel before *Enterprise* was launched in December, trucked from City Island to California, and raced there during the winter and spring. *Independence*, as she is called, is sponsored by the Kings Point Fund, designed and skippered by the other great American sailmaker, Ted Hood, and will draw upon *Courageous*' crew. Further, she will work against *Courageous*, with Ted Turner at the helm training for his own second attempt at the defense with an updated *Courageous*. *Mariner* and *Intrepid* will almost certainly be campaigned, the latter initially as a trial horse for *Enterprise*. Supersailors Dennis Conner, Graham Hall, Bill Ficker, Bill Buchan, and Gerry Driscoll offer a generous choice of possible skippers, tacticians, and the like.

The opposition is still, to some extent, nebulous. The British, having consumed £200,000 of sheep-rancher Livingstone's money in tank tests and design development, have turned the effort over to folk-hero Chay Blyth for further fund raising, organization, and supervision. If persistence is the key to victory, Blyth, who has rowed a dory across the Atlantic, should have been able to raise the funds, but he failed, his expensively designed challenger is unlofted, and a British challenge has died again.

Baron Bich's French challenge is still firm, and his aluminum Twelve is constructed and being sailed in Hyeres. In 1974, Jean-Marie Le Guillou was learning fast while losing four straight to the Australians. His sails were worse than his crew. Possibly, with extended trials before the actual elimination races, and duPont fibers for his sails, he has the essential base to develop a competitive boat. Certainly after failing in two challenges, Baron Bich now knows that prolonged competition in actual races is essential to his hopes, and he's in the fortunate position of managing the eliminations through the Yacht Club of Hyeres—an organization he virtually controls. He has suggested to all challengers a series of observation, semi-final, and final eliminations. These eliminations, to start one month after the American ones, in July, were unsettled as to details in February 1977. The Australian and Swedish negotiants were understandly reluctant to commit themselves to the decisions of an arbitrary selection committee, which the NYYC, managing the American trials, has historically been.

Starting their trials a month after the NYYC, and tilting toward a point-scoring selection process, in which one accumulates virtue, like equity, instead of discovering the true gold of ultimate success, they seem to be moving only midway toward the American development process, and, unfortunately, only half away from the uninstructive finality of the traditional best-four-out-of-seven series.

The Australians overspent in 1974 and found money very tight in 1976–7. Bond, maximizing his press coverage by an off-again, on-again series of announcements, added John Valentijn to his design team, thus bringing Bob Miller from the cut-and-try age to the computer age. Valentijn joined Bond's team fresh from several years at Sparkman & Stephens, and must have brought with him considerable knowledge of The State of the Twelve-meter Art. So Bond must also have an "ultimate twelve." Bond's boat was framed and plated by January 1977, but there is no indication that his crew and sail problems will be fewer than in 1974. Since Jim Hardy's *Matilda* syndicate failed to raise sufficient funds, another Aussie challenge will come from Olympic medalist Gordon Ingate, with a redesigned *Gretel II*, aluminum-decked and with increased sail area. Alan Payne is Ingate's designer, and is the only designer to take races from the defenders. Quite plainly he is on to something, for the rebuilt *Gretel II* is longer and lighter than Bond's and Packer's *Gretel II*, and, no doubt, better. Further Payne's new mast is designed for extensive manipulation of sail-shape.

The Swedish challenge appears currently to be

233

the most realistic. It will be directed by Pelle Petterson, who, like Ted Hood, is a designer, sailmaker, and a supersailor—World's Star champion and Olympic medalist. He has been called "the first world-class sailor ever to helm a challenger" by no less a judge than our own Dennis Conner. He is the same age and height as Hood, and, like Ted, produces a line of boats of his own design which are the best selling in Sweden—the Maxi line of cruising boats.

Sverige was completed and launched on September 1, 1976, and has been sailing against the S & S altered *Columbia*. Like Hood's *Independence*, she's a small, light Twelve. Unlike *Independence*, she has both a shortened waterline and a decreased sail area. Her entry has been blunted to decrease her waterline measurement there, and her transom cut away flat to well under her counter, to accomplish the same shortening of measurement. Her underbody, well shrouded at her launch, probably concealed a severe hollowing of the characteristic deep "V" section common to recent Twelves. Petterson's plan is to win the America's Cup with a light displacement easily driven boat. Extensive tank tests and explorations of the rule with Volvo's computers have undoubtedly reduced his wetted surface, given him shape rather than ballasted stiffness, and made his keel conformation slimmer and more efficient. With good sails and effective tactics, he will do well in modest airs to weather, and be a real threat off the wind. Newport's chopped-up seas, however, need weight and length. Petterson owns the North Sails loft for Sweden, so out of the bewildering array of choices, he will use not only the same duPont fibers (which have been ruled a "raw material") as North, but also a fairly extensive background of sailmaking theory. Providing, of course, that North (North America) tells North (Sweden). Initially, Petterson will steerwith a tiller, a clear indication to many of his limited experience in large boats, particularly large boats whose steering is as cranky as a modern Twelve's. Further, in the leaving-no-stone-unturned line, Petterson is continuing his tank tests to find any additional method by which he can improve *Sverige*'s performance.

The Swedish challenge is the most nationalistic and commercial challenge in America's Cup history. Its patron is King Olaf; the chairman of the governing board of the syndicate is the Director of International Economic Affairs in the Swedish Ministry of Finance. The other seven members of the Governing Board represent Volvo, Molnlycke Marin AB (a boatbuilding concern), a bank, and two other boat companies. Volvo's computers assisted in the design of sails and hull.

The strongest threat yet to American supremacy is mounted, and the elimination series, like the American trials, will pit one challenger against another for the long summer. The early mistakes of previous challengers will thus be almost automatically eliminated by the nature of the competition and the need to lay responsibility on a skipper, to train a crew, to use the best sails and develop them.

The American defense, started twelve months earlier than ever, will be stronger than ever. *Independence* is the word for Hood, and I'm sure that he has brought the current thinking that hulls cannot be improved much more. Certainly 1974 established the fact that the ultimate Twelve was pretty much with us. The "breakthrough" tank tests were disproved. *Intrepid, Southern Cross, Courageous,* and *Mariner II,* sailed with the same depth of experience, equal sails, and equal savvy, would have been as highly competitive, one with another, as *Intrepid/West* and *Courageous.* Hood's new design will look like *Courageous,* with a slightly less inflated "V" under her middle, and a slightly less-emphasized break between the full underwater shape and the leaner out-of-water shape in the stern. Her bow will be a trifle more full. She will be, in short, a marriage between a Hood ocean racer and *Courageous,* with a middle-of-the-road hull, retreating another tiny step from the bustle.

Hood has already had a full summer of racing his new boat against *Courageous,* skippered by a determined Ted Turner and crewed by the cream of *Mariner's* troops. In 1977, after *Courageous* is redecked and rebalanced in accordance with the changed rules, she'll train against *Independence* in whatever way Hood wants until June first. From June on, A. Lee Loomis, Jr. ("The Loom"), manager of the King's Point Syndicate, will treat *Courageous* and Turner as quite independent. He hopes to "field the two finalists in the selection trials."

Enterprise is following the line Marshall suggested in his heuristic talks during the 1974 campaign. He and Lowell North have steadily attempted to turn the instinctive, descriptive art of sailmaking into a science. Computerized sail design allows performance statistics to be tested against dimensions, and North began to take the numbers a step further. The *America Jane III* experience would seem to indicate that matching the sails to the boat as well as to each other is a productive area; and since current sailcloth is undergoing a more rapid progressive development than anything else on a Twelve, sails are necessarily changing. North is now involved in a method of testing hull shapes by computer which will enable him to analyze more effectively the computerized evaluation of hull design. The new technique can predict the forward thrust and side thrust of a given sail design. To know how this complex variable will relate to the changing center of lateral resistance in a moving hull should suggest combinations of sail factors that will result in more speed made good to windward.

So *Enterprise* was tested with a twenty-two-foot instead of a nine-foot model, and Pederick and North may well be moving toward "fourth generation" sails. But they may also be moving into the science trap—the faith in statistics that turns down the fire of intuition. Ted Hood designed *Independence* without tank tests, just as he has designed seven generations of successful America's Cup sails by feel and eye. "Since 1967 (and Olin Stephens's *Intrepid*)," Hood has said, "we seem to have gone backward in hull design." The science trap is, after all, merely a subdivision of the American blind faith in what Tocqueville, two hundred years ago, called "a belief in indefinite perfectability. . . ." The converse of this is the conviction that the ultimate Twelve may have been built, and not merely once and by one country.

Through a sequence of hulls, the "twelve meter section" has evolved. Early Twelves, like *Vim* and the original *Columbia,* have a wineglass midship cross-section. The sides come down straight for a bit, swing in, and then curve back to the vertical and form the keel. Then, hull by hull, the Stephens-designed Twelves (*Constellation, Intrepid, Valiant, Courageous*) opened the curve at the waterline and carried it deeper and deeper in an inflated "V," with a less and less slabsided keel. Two rudders, the one behind the deep keel called a "trim-tab," appeared first on *Constellation.* Next came the "kicker," a sort of shallow keel running from above the "trim-tab" to a tiny steering rudder well aft. All these developments made the boats faster. Then came the marginal "improvements." First, since a longer waterline makes a boat faster, the hull came out of the water early, but ran forward close to the water all the way to the "knuckle bow," so that a bow wave produced immersion the full length of the hull and a longer waterline. Next, with DeSaix's discovery of the separation effect, the fullness of the hull was moved farther aft to move the quarter-wave aft.

The Universal Rule, under which twelve meter yachts are measured, is a complex equation which must give an answer, when the yacht's measurements are fed into it, of twelve meters. One factor works off against another, so that, in effect, a boat can be anything from all hull and no sails to all sails and no hull. The first measurement that finds out how big the hull is, is taken by a vertical "chain girth" measurement amidships (so that filling in from the turn of the bilge to the bottom of the keel does not increase any measurement). The waterline length, from the foremost point of immersion when the yacht is floating on her benchmarks in calm water, to her rudderpost, is a multiplier. The quartergirth measurement is another chain girth, one-quarter of the way aft from the bow to amidships, so a boat would measure no bigger if she were suddenly to swell like a bottlenose dolphin from this point aft. And aft, a final chain girth is taken, about at the rudderpost. Any fullness beyond the rudderpost costs sail area, so that however far aft the fullness is drawn to bring the "separation" aft, it has to be resolved to zero underwater by

238

the rudderpost, and anything that can reduce the measurement out of water is welcomed.

In 1970, all the new boats exploited an exaggeration of the fullness aft, and all tank-tested well. But Olin Stephens, convinced that Chance–*Intrepid* wasn't as fast as the original, and with the unwelcome experience of *Valiant*'s slow acceleration out of tacks and excessively unresponsive steering, went away from the bustle in *Intrepid III* and *Courageous*. In 1974 Stephens' effort got the fullness without the abrupt termination of the 1970 effort. Chance went in the other direction, filled *Mariner* out and cut her off square in two steps, one above the trim-tab, one above the rudder. Both Chance and Miller swelled out their latest creations directly behind the forward quartergirth measurement. The transition was smoother in *Courageous*. When *Mariner* was rebuilt, she went even farther away than Stephens from the bustle, a response that is in itself a kind of confession. Essentially, because a big hull will sail faster than a small hull, the final area to attack, when all others have been explored, is how to swell the boat without swelling the measurements, because a designer can't throw away sail area to get a bigger boat and retain enough light-air performance. The vaunted introduction of aluminum made *Mariner*'s quick rebuild possible, but it didn't really lighten or stiffen the Twelves. *Intrepid,* modified in wood and aluminum, was the lightest boat in 1974.

The secret of winning the 1974 races lay, not in breakthrough design, but in the careful exploitation of every area for moving an already "ultimate" hull by better tactics, equipment, and technique. Sparkman & Stephens, with two boats, two syndicates, rival sailmakers, and crews and skippers that combined the most extensive match-racing experience in America, stuck with a good game plan and developed two potential winners.

The principles that underlay their success were clear and simple. First, they had separate specialists responsible for each specialty, and developed superior techniques in that specialty: Marshall's gathering the controls of the sails forward where he could trim without passing orders; the concentration of one helmsman on

boat speed, one tactician on tactics; the tremendously precise performance of Herreshoff as navigator, assisted by "Sidney Greybox." Second, the concept that a yacht race is not aggression, but problem solving. A race is a set of variables, of capabilities. Much is made of the importance of the start, and rightly. But winning the start, like everything else in a contest, comes from seeing the problem an opponent presents and thinking of a solution to it. A winner is a man who never runs dry of ideas; your adversary is not your opponent, but your capacity. There are different solutions for different variables. *Intrepid* found she couldn't break through *Courageous'* cover, so she stayed to weather of *Courageous,* tempting her to pinch and thus slip off, and *Intrepid* tacked west, toward lifts. Hood licked that tactic by clapping on a closer cover, and, once ahead, tacking away from *Intrepid* to the west, and back toward her. In short, to beat a match-racing opponent, a succession of challenges to his basic behavior must be mounted. The third and final advantage of the American approach is its depth of management experience. Both syndicates put in a management oar when

they felt it was needed. *Courageous* had North sails bought for her and put aboard. I'm sure that this sort of input, outside the immediate team context, put DuMoulin and Conner aboard *Intrepid* and *Courageous*. Hints, questions, and conferences kept development channels open and accomplished a depth of exploration beyond that of a one-man challenge. An experienced syndicate, so far, has belonged to the United States alone.

Our advantages, still great and substantially unchallenged, are slowly diminishing. With a French, a Swedish, and two Australian boats working through elimination races with each other, 1977's challenger will, for the first time, be tempered in competition. The Swedish challenge will have all the advantages an inexperienced syndicate can bring; the Australian and French challenges will bring more Cup experience to the line than any previous challengers. All the new designs will favor better light-air performance; all will be essentially "ultimate" Twelves and competitive. Yet, for still another series, the Americans will almost certainly win because the game suits them so well.

No two roses are the same, but seasonally the miracle happens all over again. Out of a long crossbreeding and a wide spreading of the seed, the bare bush rises, the leaves spring, and some force bursts the flower from the bud. The world has no certainties and many miracles. One is that men demonstrate lasting truths in their games, because any lasting game actualizes the instinctive values of a culture; and the more elaborate and compelling the game, the more it epitomizes those values. In the Twelves, the subtle marriage of a skipper's instincts and trained touch are coordinated with a delegation of responsibility and a dependence on sailtrimmer, tactician, navigator, foredeck boss, and crew. The whole beautiful performance leans further on corporate support, committee analysis, and deep faith in the success of a search for a better sail, a smoother hull, more effort, faster decisions, and better problem solving.

The minor design changes in the current crop of Twelves recognize the importance of problem solving, decision making, and tactics. When *Sverige*, *Enterprise*, and *Gretel II* were launched, their after ends were shrouded from vulgar eyes.

Possibly the questions raised by such secrecy are answered in forerunner Hood's areas of attack: better maneuvering, and better airflow over his sails. *Independence* was launched with no skeg, a bigger trim-tab, and a shorter keel. Using the trim-tab together with the rudder for all steering, she handled more graciously than any recent Twelve, and gained *Courageous* coming out of every tack. Her mast, tapered to balance without any added weight, utilizes all its metal for strength. It is slimmer aloft than any previous Twelve and has no jumpers. Strawberry shaped in section, with the sail going up in a slot where the stem would be, it achieves cleaner airflow than any previous mast. It will also bend more consistently than any previous American mast, and thus offer better control of sail shape. From this evidence one concludes that Ted expects close maneuvering, vital starts, intense competition on the course—both in contending for the defense, and in handling the challenger.

Americans have grown up since the day when a few privileged opportunists at the New York Yacht Club did their bit to boost national ego and win the Cup by making sure the rules gave them gross advantage. It moved through a dull era where it was a mere exercise of the privileged few, an exhibition like the vast Newport "cottages." It is passing from the time, as the contest grows keener, when it is "like IBM" and the advantage is to American technological superiority, to a time where excellence can rise to triumph wherever it comes from.

This is the dawn of a new era. Both sides will have equal time in competition. Governments have seen fit to view the contest as tax-deductible. The most socialized democratic government in Europe is sponsoring a national industrial effort to lift the "auld mug"; the greenest and most exciting continent in the world is again fielding one-man, do-it-yourself challenges. The technological differences are fading, the cultural differences are fading, the values are beginning to synthesize. It's a brave new world. Yet no matter who wins the America's Cup, it symbolizes, with dignified rituals, a complex of essentially American values. And, like America's 200 years of independence, The Cup's 107 years of continued residence at the New York Yacht Club constitute a proud challenge to the world.

1958, SEVENTEENTH DEFENSE, *Columbia* — *Sceptre*

America's Cup Committee of the New York Yacht Club:
W. A. W. Stewart, *Chairman*

Harold S. Vanderbilt, Henry S. Morgan, George R. Hinman, Luke B. Lockwood, Charles F. Havemeyer, J. Burr Bartram

	Defender, *Columbia*	Challenger, *Sceptre*
LOA	69'7"	70'
LWL	45'	44'
Beam	12'	12'
Draft	8'11"	8'11"
SA	1985	2000
Disp.	56,800	68,000
Ballast	–	–
Owner	Sears Syndicate, Henry Sears, Gerard B. Lambert, Briggs S. Cunningham, William T. Moore, A. Howard Fuller, James A. Farrell, Jr.—NYYC	Royal Yacht Squadron Syndicate, Hugh Goodson, Lord Runciman, Lt. Col. Arthur Acland, H. A. Andreae, Viscount Camrose, B. Currie, Group-Capt. Loel Guiness, Maj. H. W. Hall, Sir Peter Hoare, Maj. R. N. Macdonald-Buchanan, Charles Wainman
Designer	Sparkman & Stephens	David Boyd
Builder	Henry B. Nevins, Inc.	Alexander Robertson & Sons, Ltd.
Racing No.	US 16	K 17
Skipper	Briggs Cunningham	Lt. Comm. Graham Mann

U.S. Contenders Eliminated in Trials:

	Weatherly	*Easterner*	*Vim*
LOA	69'	65'6"	69'7"
LWL	45'6"	46'	45'
Beam	11'10"	12'	12'
Draft	8'10½"	9'	8'11"
SA	1870	1920	1916
Disp.	58,000	60,000	56,900
Ballast	36,000	40,000	35,400
Owner	Henry D. Mercer, Arnold D. Frese, Cornelius S. Walsh	Chandler B. Hovey family syndicate	John N. Matthews
Designer	Philip L. Rhodes	Ray Hunt	Sparkman & Stephens
Builder	Luders Marine Construciton Co.	Graves Yacht Yard	Henry B. Nevins, Inc.
Racing No.	US 17	US 18	US 15
Skipper	Arthur Knapp, Jr.	Charles Hovey, Chandler Hovey, Jr.	Don Matthews

1958, SEVENTEENTH DEFENSE, *Columbia — Sceptre*

Record of Races:

Date	Name	Course	Wind	Time of start	Time of finish
9/20/58	Columbia	Windward-lee-	N½E	12.30.10	17.43.56
	Sceptre	ward twice	8 mph	12.30.11	17.51.40
		around; 24 miles			
9/22/58	Columbia	Triangular;	N½E	12.21.32	Time limit
	Sceptre	24 miles	7 mph	12.21.34	expired—
					No race
9/24/58	Columbia	Triangular;	SW½W	12.20.03	15.37.43
	Sceptre	24 miles	8–10 mph	12.20.05	15.49.25
9/25/58	Columbia	Windward-lee-	SWxW¼W	12.10.05	15.19.07
	Sceptre	ward twice	15–20 mph	12.10.04	15.27.27
		around; 24 miles			
9/26/58	Columbia	Triangular;	SWxW	12.10.10	15.14.22
	Sceptre	24 miles	12–17 mph	12.10.23	15.21.27

244

1962, EIGHTEENTH DEFENSE, *Weatherly — Gretel*

America's Cup Committee of the New York Yacht Club:
Henry S. Morgan, *Chairman*

H. Irving Pratt, Chauncey Stillman, Percy Chubb II,
George E. Roosevelt, DeCoursey Fales, Henry Sears, George R. Hinman,
W. Mahlon Dickerson

	Defender, *Weatherly*	Challenger, *Gretel*
LOA	67'	69'7"
LWL	46'0"	45'
Beam	11'10"	12'
Draft	9'	9'
SA	1840	1900
Disp.	59,000	60,480
Ballast	—	—
Owner	Henry D. Mercer, Arnold	Sir Frank Packer & Syn-
	D. Frese, Cornelius S. Walsh	dicate — Royal Sydney
		Yacht Squadron
Designer	Philip L. Rhodes	Alan Payne
Builder	Luders Marine Const. Co.	Lars Halvorsen Sons
Racing No.	US 17	KA 1
Skipper	Emil "Bus" Mosbacher	Alexander "Jock" Sturrock,
		Archie Robertson

1962, EIGHTEENTH DEFENSE, *Weatherly — Gretel*

U.S. Contenders Eliminated in Trials:

	Easterner	Columbia	Nefertiti
LOA	65′6″	69′5″	67′8″
LWL	46′8″	45′6″	46′0″
Beam	11′10½″	11′10″	13′3″
Draft	9′	8′11″	9′
SA	1890	1846	1800
Disp.	63,500	56,890	59,500
Ballast	—	—	—
Owner	Chandler Hovey	Paul V. Shields	E. Ross Anderson Syndicate, Robert W. Purcell
Designer	Ray Hunt	Sparkman & Stephens, Inc.	Frederick E. "Ted" Hood
Builder	James E. Graves Little Harbor Yard	Henry B. Nevins, Inc.	James E. Graves Little Harbor Yard
Racing No.	US 18	US 16	US 19
Skipper	Ray Hunt	Cornelius "Glit" Shields, Jr.	Ted Hood

Record of Races:

Date	Name	Course	Wind	Time of start	Time of finish
9/15/62	Weatherly Gretel	Windward-leeward twice around; 24 miles	WNW 12 mph	13.10.12 13.10.26	16.23.57 16.27.43
9/18/62	Weatherly Gretel	Triangular; 24 miles	WxN 22–28 mph	12.20.17 12.20.11	15.07.45 15.06.58
9/20/62	Weatherly Gretel	Windward-leeward twice around; 24 miles	NxE 10–11 mph	12.51.24 12.50.21	17.11.16 17.19.56
9/22/62	Weatherly Gretel	Triangular; 24 miles	S½E 9–11 mph	13.05.19 13.05.23	16.27.28 16.27.54
9/25/62	Weatherly Gretel	Windward-leeward twice around; 24 miles	WSW 9–11 mph	13.10.13 13.10.09	16.26.17 16.29.57

1964, NINETEENTH DEFENSE, Constellation — Sovereign

America's Cup Committee of the New York Yacht Club:
Henry C. Morgan, Chairman

George R. Hinman, Julian K. Roosevelt, Henry Sears, Percy Chubb II, DeCoursey Fales, W. Mahlon Dickerson

	Defender, Constellation	Challenger, Sovereign
LOA	68'4"	69'
LWL	46'	45'9½"
Beam	12'	12'7"
Draft	8'10"	8'11"
SA	1800	1876
Disp.	58,411	62,000
Ballast	—	—
Owner	Constellation Syndicate — NYYC	J. Anthony Boyden — Royal Thames Yacht Club David Boyd
Designer	Sparkman & Stephens	David Boyd
Builder	Minneford Yacht Yard	Alexander Robertson & Sons
Racing No.	US 20	K 12
Skipper	Eric Ridder, Robert N. Bavier, Jr.	Peter M. Scott

U.S. Contenders Eliminated in Trials:

	Columbia	American Eagle	Easterner	Nefertiti
LOA	69'5"	68'	65'6"	67'8"
LWL	45'6"	46'	46'8"	46'
Beam	11'10"	12'	11'10½"	13'3"
Draft	8'11"	9'	9'	9'
SA	1846	1850	1890	1800
Disp.	56,890	60,000	63,500	59,500
Ballast	—	—	—	—
Owner	Thomas P. Dougan	Aurora Syndicate	Chandler Hovey	Anderson-Purcell Syndicate
Designer	Sparkman & Stephens	A. E. Luders Jr.	C. Raymond Hunt	Frederick E. Hood
Builder	Nevins Yacht Yard	Luders Marine Constr. Co.	James E. Graves, Inc.	James E. Graves, Inc.
Racing No.	US 16	US 21	US 18	US 19
Skipper	Walter Podolak	William S. Cox	Charles Hovey	Frederick E. Hood

Eliminated Challenger:

	Kurrewa V		
LOA	69'	Ballast	—
LWL	45'9½"	Owner	F. W. & J. M. Livingston
Beam	12'7"	Designer	David Boyd
Draft	8'11"	Builder	Alex. Robertson & Sons
SA	1876	Racing No.	K 3
Disp.	62,000	Skipper	Col. R. S. Perry

1964, NINETEENTH DEFENSE, *Constellation — Sovereign*

Record of Races:

Date	Name	Course	Wind	Time of start	Time of finish
9/15/64	Constellation Sovereign	1964 America's Cup Course; 24.3 nautical miles	WxS 7–9 mph	12.35.00 12.35.00	16.05.41 16.11.15
9/17/64	Constellation Sovereign	1964 America's Cup Course; 24.3 nautical miles	SSW 17–20 mph	12.10.00 12.10.00	15.56.48 16.17.12
9/19/64	Constellation Sovereign	1964 America's Cup Course; 24.3 nautical miles	E½N 15–17 mph	12.10.00 12.10.00	15.48.07 15.54.40
9/21/64	Constellation Sovereign	1964 America's Cup Course; 24.3 nautical miles	ExN 21 mph	12.10.00 12.10.00	16.22.27 16.38.07

1967, TWENTIETH DEFENSE, *Intrepid — Dame Pattie*

America's Cup Committee of the New York Yacht Club:
Henry S. Morgan, *Chairman*

Percy Chubb II, Julian K. Roosevelt, W. Mahlon Dickerson, Henry Sears, Charles Francis Adams

	Defender, *Intrepid*	Challenger, *Dame Pattie*
LOA	64'	65'2"
LWL	45'6"	46'11"
Beam	12'	11'11"
Draft	9'	9'1"
SA	1850	1795
Disp.	57,500	58,000
Ballast	—	—
Owner	Intrepid Syndicate — NYYC	Emil Christensen and America's Cup Challenger Syndicate — Royal Sydney Yacht Squadron
Designer	Sparkman & Stephens	Warwick J. Hood
Builder	Minneford Yacht Yard	William H. Barnett
Racing No.	US 22	KA 2
Skipper	Emil "Bus" Mosbacher, Jr.	Alexander "Jock" Sturrock

1967, TWENTIETH DEFENSE, *Intrepid — Dame Pattie*

U.S. Contenders Eliminated in Trials:

	American Eagle	Columbia	Constellation
LOA	68'	67'	68'4"
LWL	46'	45'6"	46'
Beam	12'	11'10"	12'
Draft	9'	8'11"	9'
SA	1850	1775	1800
Disp.	60,000	60,000	58,500
Ballast	—	—	—
Owner	American Eagle Syndicate	Thomas P. Dougan	Intrepid Syn. (charter)
Designer	A. E. Luders, Jr.	Sparkman & Stephens	Sparkman & Stephens
Builder	Luders Marine Constr. Co.	Nevins Yt. Yard	Minneford Yt. Yard
Racing No.	US 21	US 16	US 20
Skipper	George Hinman	Briggs S. Cunningham	Robert W. McCullough

Record of Races:

Date	Name	Course	Wind	Time of start	Time of finish
9/12/67	Intrepid	America's Cup Course — 24.3 nautical miles	ExN¼N	12.30.00	15.55.03
	Dame Pattie		17–21 mph	12.30.00	16.01.01
9/13/67	Intrepid	America's Cup Course — 24.3 nautical miles	ExN¼N	12.35.00	16.04.21
	Dame Pattie		8–16 mph	12.35.00	16.07.57
9/14/67	Intrepid	America's Cup Course — 24.3 nautical miles	NExE	12.20.00	15.40.14
	Dame Pattie		14–18 mph	12.20.00	15.44.55
9/18/67	Intrepid	America's Cup Course — 24.3 nautical miles	SW	14.00.00	17.27.39
	Dame Pattie		9–14 mph	14.00.00	17.31.14

1970, TWENTY-FIRST DEFENSE, *Intrepid* — *Gretel II*

America's Cup Committee of the New York Yacht Club:
Henry S. Morgan, *Chairman*

Clayton Ewing, Donald B. Kipp, Henry Sears, Percy Chubb II,
Charles Francis Adams, Julian K. Roosevelt

	Defender, *Intrepid*	Challenger, *Gretel II*
LOA	64'6"	62'
LWL	47'	46'
Beam	12'3"	12'6"
Draft	9'2"	9'6"
SA	app. 1750	app. 1750
Disp.	app. 60,000	app. 60,000
Ballast	—	—
Owner	Intrepid Syndicate — NYYC	Sir Frank Packer — Royal Sydney Yacht Squadron
Designer	S&S; re-design, Britton Chance, Jr.	Alan Payne
Builder	Minneford Yacht Yard	Billy Barnett
Racing No.	US 22	KA 3
Skipper	Bill Ficker	Jim Hardy

U.S. Contenders Eliminated in Trials:

	Heritage	Valiant	Weatherly
LOA	62'6"	63'	66'10"
LWL	50'	47'	46'
Beam	12'6"	12'	11'10"
Draft	9'4"	9'6"	8'11"
SA	1725–1750	1750	1850
Disp.	70,500	69,000	59,000
Ballast	—	—	—
Owner	Charles E. Morgan, Jr.	Valiant Syndicate	Weatherly Syndicate
Designer	Charles E. Morgan, Jr.	Sparkman & Stephens	Philip L. Rhodes
Builder	Morgan Yacht Corp.	Robert Derecktor	Luders Marine
Racing No.	US 23	US 24	US 17
Skipper	Charles E. Morgan, Jr.	Bob McCullough	George Hinman

Date	Name	Course	Wind	Time of start	Time of finish
9/15/70	Intrepid	America's Cup	109°	12.10.10	15.36.03
	Gretel II	Course — 24.3	20 kts	12.10.00	15.41.55
		nautical miles			
9/20/70	Intrepid	America's Cup	238°	14.00.00	18.38.10
	Gretel II	Course — 24.3	6 kts	14.00.00	18.37.03
		nautical miles			

Gretel II was disqualified for a foul after the starting signal and the race was awarded to Intrepid.

Date	Name	Course	Wind	Time of start	Time of finish
9/22/70	Intrepid	America's Cup	236°	12.10.00	15.34.43
	Gretel II	Course — 24.3	10 kts	12.10.00	15.36.01
		nautical miles			
9/24/70	Gretel II	America's Cup	076°	12.10.00	15.33.59
	Intrepid	Course — 24.3	10 kts	12.10.00	15.35.01
		nautical miles			
9/28/70	Intrepid	America's Cup	360°	12.10.00	16.39.03
	Gretel II	Course — 24.3	9–10 kts	12.10.00	16.40.47
		nautical miles			

1970, TWENTY-FIRST DEFENSE, Intrepid — Gretel II

Eliminated Challenger:

France

LOA	62'6"	Ballast	—
LWL	46'6"	Owner	Baron Marcel Bich
Beam	12'6"	Designer	Andre Mauric
Draft	9'	Builder	AFCA Shipyard, Pontarlier
SA	1770	Racing No.	F 1
Disp.	app. 59,400	Skipper	Louis Noverraz

1974, TWENTY-SECOND DEFENSE, *Courageous* — *Southern Cross*

America's Cup Committee of the New York Yacht Club:
Henry S. Morgan, *Chairman*

Clayton Ewing, Henry H. Anderson, Jr., Charles Francis Adams,
Percy Chubb II, James Michael, Donald B. Kipp

	Defender, *Courageous*	Challenger, *Southern Cross*
LOA	66′	67′3″
LWL	45′6″	46′8″
Beam	12′	12′4″
Draft	8′10″	9′6″
SA	1770	1811
Disp.	58,000	62,000
Ballast	—	—
Owner	Courageous Syndicate — NYYC	Alan Bond — Royal Perth Yacht Club
Designer	Sparkman & Stephens	Bob Miller
Builder	Minneford Yacht Yard	Halvorsen, Morson & Gowland
Racing No.	US 26	KA 4
Skipper	Bob Bavier	Jim Hardy

U.S. Contenders Eliminated in Trials:

	Intrepid	*Valiant*	*Mariner*
LOA	64′6″	63′	63′
LWL	47′	47′	45′
Beam	12′3″	12′	12′
Draft	9′	9′6″	9′
SA	1770	1750	1800
Disp.	60,000	69,000	62,000
Ballast	—	—	—
Owner	Seattle Sailing Foundation	U.S. Merchant Marine Academy	U.S. Merchant Marine Academy
Designer	Sparkman & Stephens	Sparkman & Stephens, Britton Chance, Jr.	Britton Chance, Jr.
Builder	Minneford Yacht Yard ('67) Driscoll Custom Boats ('73)	Robert E. Derecktor	Robert E. Derecktor
Racing No.	US 22	US 24	US 25
Skipper	Gerry Driscoll	George Hinman	Ted Turner

251

1974, TWENTY-SECOND DEFENSE, *Courageous* — *Southern Cross*

Challengers Eliminated:

	Gretel II	*France*
LOA	63'	62'6"
LWL	46'	46'6"
Beam	12'6"	12'6"
Draft	9'6"	9'
SA	1750	1770
Disp.	60,000	59,400
Ballast	—	—
Owner	Alan Bond	Baron Marcel Bich
Designer	Alan Payne	Andre Mauric
Builder	Billy Barnett	AFCA Shipyard, Pontarliers, Herman Egger
Racing No.	KA 3	F 1
Skipper	John Cuneo	Jean Marie LeGuillou

Record of Races:

Date	Name	Course	Wind	Time of start	Time of finish
9/10/74	Courageous	America's Cup	212°	14:10:06	18:22:03
	Southern Cross	Course — 24.3 nautical miles	11 kts	14:10:08	18:26:57
9/12/74	Courageous	America's Cup	237°	12:10:09	15:42:57
	Southern Cross	Course — 24.3 nautical miles	11 kts	12:10:08	15:43:48
9/14/74	Race 3 was started but due to light wind neither yacht finished within the time limit which expired at 17:40. *Southern Cross* requested a layover day the next day.				
9/16/74	Courageous	America's Cup	305°	12:11:01	15:43:02
	Southern Cross	Course — 24.3 nautical miles	12 kts	12:11:17	15:48:29
9/17/74	Courageous	America's Cup	109°	12:10:07	15:42:25
	Southern Cross	Course — 24.3 nautical miles	12 kts	12:10:27	15:49:44